Praise for *How to Say It® to Girls* by Nancy Gruver

"If you're serious about raising a daughter who believes she can do and be anything, you'll want Nancy Gruver in your corner. From the creator of the best girls' magazine out there comes **the best parenting book out there**. *How To Say It® to Girls* is an A to Z primer for growing a girl who's smart, strong, and brave."

> —Lyn Mikel Brown, Ed.D., associate professor, Colby College, and author of *Girlfighting: Betrayal and Rejection Among Girls*

"Veteran girl expert Nancy Gruver serves up a boundless smorgasbord for parents of girls that will stay fresh from toddler through teen years. **Readers will keep returning to this resource-packed bible** for hundreds of age-appropriate conversation starters, thoughtful overviews, and info treasure troves for dozens of parenting issues."

> —Helen Cordes, author of *Girl Power in the Mirror*

"With clarity and comprehensiveness, Nancy Gruver offers parents an extraordinarily practical, down-to-earth primer that **should grace the library of every caring mom and dad of a young girl**. One comes away from reading this gem of a book with handy pearls of wisdom that will undoubtedly enhance every parent's daughter-raising ability."

> —Rev. Steve Emmett, Ph.D., co-founder of The Renfrew Center

"**Looking for a way to 'reach' your daughter? You found it.** This practical guide for parents teaches us what to say (and just as importantly, what not to say). I wish I had this book when my own daughters were growing up."

> —David Sadker, American University, School of Education

"With the pressures facing girls today, loving our daughters is not enough. More than ever, parents have to understand these pressures and know how to cut through the noise to actively help girls stay connected to who they are inside. With Nancy Gruver's boundless warmth and contemporary wisdom, *How To Say It® to Girls* **gives parents inspiration, courage, and the right words** to say or *not* to say to keep the channels open."

> —Kathy Kater, LICSW, author of *Real Kids Come in All Sizes: Ten Essential Lessons to Build Your Child's Body Esteem*

"All parents deal with a wide array of challenges as they raise their daughters from newborns to young ladies, and this book is an excellent resource during difficult times. **Keep this book in a safe place. You'll be referring to it often.**"

> —Bill Klatte MSW, ACSW

"Essential reading for anyone parenting a girl, this comprehensive, accessible, and sparkling compendium provides pertinent and practical advice wherever the pages fall open. The alphabetically arranged topics and the sections with age-appropriate advice are as useful as the lists of what to say and what not to say. **Keep this book on your nightstand until your girl grows up . . . and needs it herself!**"

    —Rosalie Maggio, author of *How to Say It*®

"There has never been a better time for a book like [this], as the struggle to raise healthy and confident girls grows ever more complex and challenging. **This book is a timely gift** to all parents and anyone who works with children."

    —Margaret Willey, author of *The Bigger Book of Lydia* and *Clever Beatrice*

"*How to Say It*® *to Girls* is **a wonderful compilation of strategies and resources that will** help parents and girls reach their fullest potential . . . together."

    —Dale McCreedy, Ph.D., director, Gender and Family Learning Programs
    Franklin Institute Science Museum

"A straightforward guide that will help us deal with the everyday issues, such as embarrassment and chores, as well as with the real toughies, such as morality and death. Gruver's advice is solid and practical, giving parents the words to use and actions to take along with those we should avoid."

    —Harriet S. Mosatche, Ph.D., author of *Getting to Know the Real You: 50 Fun Quizzes*
    Just for Girls

"The amazing Nancy Gruver demonstrates once again that she is a skillful advocate for girls and their families. This book tells us how to talk with girls respectfully and joyfully, how to listen and learn from them, and how to join them in changing the world for the better."

    —Heather Johnston Nicholson, Ph.D., director of research, Girls Incorporated®

HOW TO SAY IT®
to Girls

Communicating with Your
Growing Daughter

NANCY GRUVER

PRENTICE HALL PRESS

Prentice Hall Press
Published by The Berkley Publishing Group
A division of Penguin Group (USA) Inc.
375 Hudson Street
New York, New York 10014

Copyright © 2004 by Nancy Gruver
Cover design by Jill Boltin
Illustrations by Paul Howalt
Text design by Tiffany Estreicher

First Prentice Hall Press paperback edition: October 2004

ISBN: 0-7352-0385-7

Visit our website at
www.penguin.com

Library of Congress Cataloging-in-Publication Data

Gruver, Nancy.
    How to say it to girls / by Nancy Gruver.—1st Prentice Hall Press pbk. ed.
       p. cm.
    ISBN 0-7352-0385-7
    1. Mothers and daughters—Psychology. 2. Communication in the family. 3. Parenting.
4. Developmental psychology. I. Title.

    HQ755.85.G78 2004
    649'.125—dc22   2004054495

Printed in the United States of America

10 9 8 7 6 5 4 3 2 1

TABLE OF CONTENTS

ACKNOWLEDGMENT

The learning that went into this book started twenty-four years ago with my daughters, Mavis and Nia. They were my motivation for finding better ways to communicate with girls. The combination of their trust and high expectations kept me working to improve our communication. Now that they're adults, the deep joy of our closeness continues to reward all the experimentation and difficult conversations along the way.

For the past twelve years, communicating well with girls has been my work as well as my passion. I'm deeply grateful to the many people who have shared their knowledge, insight, frustrations and experience with me in this work. Extra special thanks are due to all the girls who have been part of *New Moon* Magazine's Girls Editorial Board. You have showed me over and over again how strong communication is the foundation for everything we can accomplish together. Likewise, my adult colleagues at *New Moon* magazine and *Daughters* newsletter have been irreplaceable partners in creating and refining ways to share power with girls so they can share their voices with the world. In addition, they literally made it possible for me to take the time to write.

The girls who read *New Moon* and the adults who read *Daughters* newsletter are the inspiration for my ongoing work. You helped me choose the topics to cover here and your stories and questions are woven throughout. Your encouragement and constructive criticism keep teaching me every day. Thank you for placing your trust in what we do.

Friends and serendipity played a big role in making this book a reality. Rosalie Maggio both suggested that I write it and persuaded the series editor, Tom Power of Prentice Hall, that I was the right person to do it. Tom helped me refine my ideas and we were on the verge of a contract when the Penguin group bought Prentice Hall. The project might have died at that point but for literary agent Coleen O'Shea's intervention when John Duff of Penguin showed her my proposal. Coleen and I knew each other from college but had lost touch. Her call rekindled our friendship and she guided me through the contract and writing process. Editor Michelle Howry was encouraging, questioning and patient as the book evolved and changed. She provided just enough nudging to get me over the finish line and then increased the clarity and usefulness of the book through her editing.

Joe Kelly has been my partner in both raising our daughters and building *New Moon* magazine and *Daughters* newsletter. Committing his extraordinary energy and creativity to our family and this work is a most wonderful gift. We've shared the ups and downs of parenting and small business. Joe has also been my informal writing coach for many years, building my confidence in my written voice and perspective. In all the ways that count most, this book owes a great deal to his unfaltering support and help.

INTRODUCTION

One of my favorite motherhood moments happened when my twin daughters were sixteen years old. Nia was struggling to make a decision. Even though I knew what I thought she should do, I was keeping that to myself. With a purposely open and non-committal look on my face, I listened to her review the pros and cons, at great length. Several times I stopped myself from interjecting, contenting myself instead with some measured head nods and carefully timed "hmmmms" to let her know that I was listening. Soon I found myself thinking what a good mom I was to just listen and not give unsolicited advice like my mom had. As Nia talked, I silently patted myself on the back and mused about how I had finally gotten the hang of not trying to solve my girls' problems for them.

All of a sudden there was a silence. I realized I hadn't actually been listening to Nia. Nevertheless, I focused on her expectant face and, with full confidence, delivered the pièce de résistance: "Honey, I know you'll make the right decision. You're really good at figuring things out." I was just about to resume my self-congratulatory reverie on the rewards of listening to girls when I saw Nia's expression turn to exasperation. Obviously, this wasn't a good sign, but I couldn't figure out what I'd done wrong now. I'd been patient and understanding and quiet, all behaviors that had not come naturally to me before motherhood. What more could she want?

"Mom, I want your *advice*! That's why I'm asking you. You actually give pretty good advice most of the time."

You could have knocked me over with a feather. My sixteen-year-old daughter was annoyed because I wasn't giving her advice! What an unexpected turn of events. And

I wasn't ready for it since I hadn't been listening closely to her. In fact, I had to admit that and ask her to repeat her thinking so I could really pay attention and then tell her what I thought. Even with that humbling reality, it was one of the most meaningful compliments I've ever received.

This experience showed me that years of improving communication had brought us to a place I couldn't imagine before we were there. My teenage daughter both knew her own mind and felt enough confidence in it to want to know my opinion. She trusted herself to make the final decision. She also trusted that I would tell her things that could help her make a good decision. And she trusted me to support her, even if her decision wasn't what I recommended. I hadn't reached this kind of relationship with my mother until I was well into my thirties and a mother myself.

The journey of raising girls is a rich and unexpected one. It takes us deep into ourselves, as well as out into the world, in ways we can never fully imagine until they happen. Our daughters have provided me and my husband with our greatest challenges and our most rewarding experiences. Every time we thought we had it figured out, something happened to remind us that the essence of parenting is continuous learning, both about our daughters and about ourselves. This is especially true with communication. We're usually grateful for that, when we're not exhausted by it!

As the founder and publisher of *New Moon: The Magazine for Girls and Their Dreams*, I also am told by thousands of other girls what they need and expect from the adults in their lives. Hearing about them and from them has given me the great gift of awareness and respect for girls and what they know. It has also shown me just how much girls need from adults. They depend on us to really know them and to do what's best for them. Deep down, they want us to provide them with informed and loving guidance. This doesn't mean preaching. And it doesn't mean they are always grateful for it in the moment!

Raising girls and boys has many common experiences, hurdles, and rewards. But there are also key differences based on gender that require parents to know the special nuances of guiding a girl rather than a boy. Even today, girls and boys face different expectations and limitations beginning as early as infancy. Research shows that little girls are taught more social interaction skills and little boys are taught more physical skills. And that's only the simplest aspect of how girls and boys are treated differently in our culture. In order to provide the best support and guidance, we need to be informed about both developmental gender differences and the varying affects of social realities on girls and boys. That's why this book focuses specifically on girls' development, needs, and key issues from birth to adolescence.

You'll find that many of the key issues discussed here are important throughout girlhood, although not in the same way at each stage. Most parents feel the greatest need for communication help with their daughter during adolescence, which seems to be starting earlier and earlier—socially, emotionally, and biologically. But it's important to remember that building the solid foundation of strong communication can begin long before puberty exerts its pressure. In fact, every effort we put into improving communication and understanding with our preadolescent daughters will repay us amply during the most difficult times. You'll notice that I emphasize different aspects of certain issues for different ages. These age-specific approaches build the foundation during each girl's childhood, setting each block upon the preceding one in a way that strengthens the whole, by being in tune with her emotional and intellectual development.

I have found that adults have much to learn from girls. Until the preteen years, most girls have an inspiring emotional directness and openness. They know who they are in a very immediate way. Even more important, they are comfortable being themselves. Their inner selves and their outer actions are directly connected, seemingly without effort. They expect the world to be a just place, and they expect themselves and others to act with integrity and caring. Their clear vision of the shortcomings of the world and humanity—"That's not fair!"—doesn't make them cynical. Instead, it makes them want to change things, expecting the best. And they feel powerful enough to do so, against all logical odds. All these things are great examples for adults about how to live our convictions, with heart and soul, in a world that can be discouraging. In so many ways, adults have as much to gain from better communication with girls as girls themselves do.

In raising my daughters and working with many other girls, I've found a few simple steps to improve communication between adults and girls. Conveniently, these steps spell out the word *GIRLS*. You'll see how applying these steps can lead to more effective and satisfying communication, for you and for your daughter. Every step doesn't need to be used in every situation. Each situation is unique, depending on the girl, on you, and on many other factors. Only you and she can decide what helps. Trial and error is encouraged. As they say in 12-step programs, "Take what you need and leave the rest."

"G" is for Get to Know Her. In order to communicate effectively with girls, we need to know who they really are. We get to know girls by spending time with them, doing the things they want to do. This means having their friends around and getting to know them. It means driving the car pool, marveling at what we learn from listening to the conversations. It means playing the games a girl likes to play, listening to music she likes, and watching movies and TV shows she watches. It means reading the books and magazines she reads. It means volunteering to coach her team, lead her scout troop, go on field trips, or help her build a tree house—even if we're not the least bit interested in those activities on their own.

It means asking her what she thinks about all kinds of things, small and big. It means accepting her for who she is and not trying to get her to be a different person. It means valuing her special gifts and helping her find the way to bring those gifts out in daily life. It also means acknowledging the many things she knows about herself and the world and valuing her knowledge. Girls know when we really know them, and then they take what we have to say much more seriously. It only makes sense.

"I" is for Improvise and Ignore Stereotypes. There is no one way for everyone. Every girl and every adult brings his or her own special knowledge, style, and needs to communication. It's important to embrace this fact and not fight it. While this book is full of useful suggestions about how to communicate effectively with girls, none of them are "the only right way." Read them over and see if you think they fit. See if they fit you, if they fit the girl, if they fit the situation. If they don't exactly fit, then feel free to alter them until they feel right. Improvising requires us to trust our own instincts and gut feelings. Bring your creativity and problem solving to bear on the challenge at hand. The mere act of focusing your energy on improving communication does a world of good.

Ignoring stereotypes is another aspect of fitting communication to the people and the situation. Our minds create stereotypes as a way to help us understand the world. When we assign a stereotype to a girl—i.e., "She's a 'nice' girl." "She's a tomboy." "She's boy crazy."—we reduce the complexity of her self to shorthand notation. No person, and certainly no growing girl, is that simplistic. Trying to squeeze her into a stereotype is a disservice, and it puts a huge roadblock in the way of communicating. Stereotypes put blinders on our perception and prevent us from seeing the whole complex picture of who she is and what's happening with her right now. In order to communicate well, we need to be open to all of her. Admittedly, this is not always easy. But it's always worthwhile.

"R" is for Remember Who She Is. Remember who your daughter really is, regardless of how she's acting right now. Her development is a continuum, not a series of unrelated events. It's important to remind girls of their special strengths and experiences, especially at difficult times. Using our memories and perspective, we can help her re-connect to her inner self and find the path that's uniquely right for her. Girls can lose sight of their truest selves and their goals, particularly in the preteen and teen years, due to the immense pressures of trying to meet our culture's expectations of them. They are still maturing and don't have fully developed adult thinking and emotions to help them maintain perspective. So it's part of our role to help with that. When we know a girl well, we see who she now is as a continuation of who she was months and years ago, not as a whole different person. Using this perspective can help girls connect what they see as a "new self " to the inner self they have been all along. We can provide the link to the inner self that helps a girl maintain a sense of wholeness and trust in herself.

"L" is for Listen. Be right there with her, wherever she is at the moment that she's communicating with you. Truly listening to another person is the greatest communication challenge humans face. And this challenge can be even more crucial with girls. Girls have a "relationship radar" that alerts them quickly when we're not really listening. When they know we're not really listening, they may react several ways. Most helpfully, they can tell us that they know we're not listening: "You don't get it," or "You don't understand anything!" or "You don't even care!" What these phrases really mean are "I don't feel heard," or "You're not listening." What matters here is that she feels heard. And so if a girl is able to provide coaching by letting us know when she doesn't feel listened to, we are well advised to accept the coaching and ask for feedback on how to show her that we're listening.

A much less helpful (for her and us) response is for her to just subtly shut down and get quiet ("It's nothing," "It doesn't really matter," or "Never mind") or to change what she's saying to see if that will get us to listen. She might say something she thinks will shock us, or she might just talk about unimportant things. In either case, we've lost an opportunity to hear her deepest feelings and thoughts. At the same time, we've given her the message that her deepest feelings and thoughts are unimportant, which may encourage her to "forget" them. And that means that communication between us will get harder and less satisfying. If she gets quiet and shuts down, it's our job to recognize the signals and take action to drastically improve our sincere listening. We may need to make repeated efforts to initiate communication and demonstrate that we really will listen before she will start taking the initiative to tell us things again. Successful listening is the absolute minimum requirement for effective communication with a girl.

"S" is for Share Ourselves and Our Knowledge. Girls want to really know the important adults in their lives. They want to know our good sides and our bad sides. But it can be very hard for adults to be fully honest about ourselves with girls. We worry that they will think less of us or that they can't handle knowing the truth about us or things we've done. We think that perhaps they will take advantage of our mistakes and short-comings and use them to manipulate us. However, when we are really honest with girls about ourselves, warts and all, in an appropriate way, respecting their age and their level of maturity, we make ourselves virtually manipulation proof.

Paradoxically, by being open and vulnerable, we build the deep trust that makes it possible for them to be honest with us. This trust also vastly increases the chance that they will listen to the knowledge we have and want so much to share with them. There's no doubt that girls need our greater knowledge of the world and its workings to help them navigate successfully. They also need the supportive people and resources that we can connect them with because we are adults. The best way to increase the chance that a girl will be open to our help when she most needs it is to be honest about who we are and what we've done and let her know all the facets of our true selves.

How It Works

While raising girls, we can reconnect with parts of our own experience that have been lost to the past. For women, rediscovering our girlhood can be exhilarating and painful at the same time. Often, we've forgotten things for a reason. Spending time with girls can bring emotional memories—both good and bad—back with breathtaking power.

I experienced this when my daughters were in eighth grade. They complained that two of their friends were "acting like they're too cool for us." Mavis's and Nia's feelings were deeply hurt by the rejection, and they felt betrayed that things were changing. I tried to convince them that they shouldn't care what these two girls did. Real friends didn't do these things, I advised, so they should just ignore them.

But that advice didn't cut it. When they said, "You don't understand!" and didn't immediately cheer up, I got impatient and felt rejected myself, wondering why they didn't trust that I knew (oh, so well) what I was talking about.

I knew firsthand that insecurity was at the root of "being cool" and abandoning old friends. Their friend troubles zapped me right back to my miserable eighth grade year when *I* suddenly became "too cool" for my longtime friends. *I* was the mean and fickle one, hurting others' feelings without regard. But I hadn't ever told my girls this story because it was painful to remember and admit how mean I'd been to my friends. I still felt guilty. And I didn't want to admit the unflattering truth. We often do this with girls. We tell them part of the truth about our experiences and ourselves but leave out some key part because it's painful to remember or we're ashamed and regret how we acted. This erects an emotional barrier that girls feel.

They can tell we're not being fully honest with them, while constantly expecting them to be honest with us. The inevitable result is distrust. Girls feel preached at, rather than understood, and the gulf between us grows. When I eventually took a deep breath and told my daughters the whole truth, they listened intently. It didn't solve their problem or take away their pain, but it did restore the bond of trust and intimacy between us. And unexpectedly, it helped me, after twenty-seven years, to forgive myself for being the insecure girl who was mean to her friends.

This is the kind of reward that effective communication with girls brings to us and them. It deepens and strengthens our relationship and helps us provide support when it's most needed.

Enjoy the Journey

Raising a daughter provides countless learning opportunities and challenges. Ideally, both we and our child grow in the process and develop a deeper understanding and respect for ourselves and each other. Often, it's the roughest spots that teach us the most and provide the greatest rewards as we work through them. Trust yourself and your daughter and just keep communicating. You'll be surprised by the ups as well as the downs, but the journey is the real point.

Other parents love to hear about your journey and share theirs. Join the free Care About Girls e-mail list by e-mailing: careaboutgirls-subscribe@yahoogroups.com

ADVENTURE

"Carolyn is cautious and hesitant about trying new things like swimming and going to sleepaway camp. I think she misses out on a lot and I want her to enjoy new things."—Shari

Things to Consider

Doing something new, challenging, or unusual for the sheer joy of it creates experiences that stick with us for our entire lives. Encouraging her to challenge and stretch herself through age-appropriate new experiences helps your daughter to feel confident about her ability to cope with unexpected things later on. Different girls seem to be born with different tolerances for adventure. If your daughter greets the unknown with exuberance and high expectations, you'll need to guide her differently than if she avoids new experiences. If she's a natural with physical adventures but shy socially, she'll need different support from you. Keep her individuality in mind.

What to Say and Do

1–7 YEARS OLD

Be aware of your response when she does new things like climbing or going to a new house to play, and when she has small injuries or upsets.

■ You're so brave!

■ It's just a little scrape (or a little scary). It'll be better soon.

■ Let's camp out in the backyard tonight.

8–13 YEARS OLD
Encourage her to try adventurous things, doing them together when appropriate.

■ What new things do you want to try this summer?

■ I never learned to dive when I was a kid. Want to learn together?

Notice what she tries on her own, and help her see how that's adventurous and that she can also be adventurous with things that she avoids.

■ You're so good at making new friends. It can be scary.

■ I loved seeing you do the ropes course. Will you help me?

14 AND UP
Allow her to be independent in her adventures, supporting her special interests. She needs to learn by doing, even if she fails sometimes. Separate your fears as her parent from the reasonable precautions you need to teach her. Let her express fears without letting them limit what she does, and do the same yourself.

■ That climbing course is expensive. Maybe it can be your birthday present.

■ I'm so glad your group is fixing up that rundown building. Here are some masks for everyone to keep from breathing in the dust.

■ I was really homesick when I went to camp for four weeks and didn't know anyone. But that's when I got to be such good friends with Sally.

Give specific, nonjudgmental feedback on what she does.

Words and Phrases to Use

- You can do it!
- I'm confident in you.
- How will you . . . ?
- Dreams

- Fun
- Challenge
- Learning

What Not to Say and Do

Don't always tell her to play it safe, and don't make fun of her idea of adventure even if you think it's tame. Don't say,

- You could hurt yourself doing that. Are you crazy?
- Stick with what you know you can do.
- Come on, don't be a scaredy-cat!
- Looking for bugs is boring. Let's do something really exciting like water-skiing.
- It won't be what you imagine.
- Better safe than sorry.
- If you're not sure . . .

Resources

Girl Scouts of the USA: www.girlscouts.org

New Moon Adventures: www.newmoon.org/events/adventures.htm

Inspire an armchair adventurer with books about adventurous girls.

Search the Internet using keywords like "girls outdoor adventures"

ANGER

"Mary has always expressed her anger openly. She had terrible tantrums as a toddler, and now she hurts her friends' feelings without realizing it. She's starting to have trouble keeping friends. She can get angry about such little things. But when she's not angry, she's a delight to be with. How can I help her not be so angry?"—Eileen

Things to Consider

There's something pushy and out of control about an angry girl, and our first impulse is to teach her that she should "be nice." Now, there's nothing wrong with being truly nice, but there *is* something wrong with teaching girls to repress their anger rather than recognize it and do something constructive with it. There is a difference between feeling angry and taking our anger out on another person.

Anger is one of the basic human emotions; we all feel it. It's a signal that there is something wrong, either in us or in the situation. It can be a warning that we need to take seriously. Anger can motivate us to make a healthy change or to right an injustice.

What to Say and Do

1–7 YEARS OLD

Help her recognize her angry feelings and realize they are normal. Respond calmly, accept her feelings without criticism, and encourage her to express anger verbally and in physical ways that don't hurt anyone or anything.

- Are you feeling angry? Tell me about it.

- It sounds like that made you angry. What happened?

- You look angry. Let's go for a walk and talk about it.

8–13 YEARS OLD

This is the age when girls start feeling strong pressure to bury their angry feelings and "be nice," no matter how they feel. Help her stay in touch with her real feelings and develop mature ways to express them. She will also start to feel angry about things in the larger world like injustice and unfairness, even if they aren't affecting her directly.

- Angry feelings can be scary because they feel out of control. You can always tell me about your angry feelings even if you don't express them right when you first feel them.

- Angry feelings tell us that something's not quite right, but we can't always figure out what that is until we talk about our feelings with someone else.

Let her hear you talk about feeling angry yourself, and show her how you express anger without hurting yourself or others.

- I'm angry that the car isn't working. I'm going to go outside and scream for a minute.

- I'm very angry that Uncle Frank was late to pick you up and it worried you. I'm going to talk with him about it later.

Help her think about what to do after she's expressed her anger and her feelings have cooled a bit.

- You felt angry at Miranda and did a good job telling me about it. Now what do you want to do to change the situation?

- The way my boss talked to me today made me angry. I'm going to go for a bike ride now to let out some of those feelings while I think about how to talk with her about it.

- Feeling angry means there's something that needs to change. What do you think it is? What can we do to make that change?

- You're right. It's not fair that the school punished everyone for something only a few kids did. Let's write a note to the principal saying what you think would have been fair for her to do.

14 AND UP

You may feel that while your daughter is nice to everyone else, she seems to be constantly angry at you, often for no reason. Or she may seem depressed and withdrawn, which is also related to unexpressed anger. In fact, she's probably angry at a lot of things that have nothing to do with you, but home is the only place she feels safe expressing her anger without jeopardizing relationships. Help her express the anger and think about how to communicate with the people she's really angry with.

- I see that you're angry. I don't think it's really about me. Tell me about it.

- It's hard to tell friends that you feel angry with them. How about pretending I'm Ramon and telling me how you feel?

- I know you're angry that we won't let you use the car after 9 p.m. until you're seventeen. You feel ready to do that, and we're still saying no.

Maintain eye contact when she's telling you she feels angry.

Words and Phrases to Use

- Anger is normal.

- How do you feel?

- Do you want to yell really loud with me?

- Your expression looks angry.

- What do you want to do about it?

- Tell me all about it.

- I still love you, even when you're angry.

- Anger is healthy.

What Not to Say and Do

Don't deny or stifle her anger or shame her for expressing it appropriately. Don't say,

- You're not really angry.

- It's no big deal. Why are you so upset?

- It's not nice to get angry.

- Go to your room until you're not angry anymore.

Don't express your anger by slapping, hitting, breaking things, slamming doors, and so forth. Don't allow her to express her anger that way, either. Don't say,

- If he hits you, you can hit him back.

- Girls don't get angry. They're nicer than boys.

- I'm tired of hearing you complain. Just keep it to yourself.

Resources

Healthy Anger: How to Help Children and Teens Manage Their Anger by Bernard Golden. Oxford University Press, 2003.

Honor Your Anger: How Transforming Your Anger Style Can Change Your Life by Beverly Engel. John Wiley & Sons, 2003.

I'm Not Mad, I Just Hate You: A New Understanding of Mother-Daughter Conflict by Roni Cohen-Sandler and Michelle Silver. Penguin, 2000.

Raising Their Voices: The Politics of Girls' Anger by Lyn Mikel Brown. Harvard University Press, 1998.

That Makes Me Mad! by Steven Kroll, illustrated by Christine Davenier. North-South Books, 2002.

When Sophie Gets Angry—Really, Really Angry written and illustrated by Molly Bang. Scholastic, 1999.

APPEARANCE

"Sasha is only nine, and all of a sudden she's obsessed about her appearance. She asked to wear makeup to school every day! She says only the geeks aren't wearing makeup. I know that's not true. But what concerns me is that she's putting so much time and energy into worrying about how she looks and trying to look exactly like everyone else. She's a great kid and has so much to feel good about. How can we counter society's focus on superficial appearance?"—Nicholas

Things to Consider

Our culture places a very high value on appearance. This focus can be harmful to girls when they get the idea that they need to look a certain way for people to like them or care about them. It tells girls that how they look is more important than who they are or what they do.

One of the most insidious ways appearance obsession hurts girls is by the vast amount of time and effort that goes into perfecting and worrying about appearance as they get older. This is time and psychological energy that she could use to develop her interests and explore the world around her. Focusing all that energy on criticizing her own appearance is counterproductive and doesn't help her feel more competent or valued. Because girls are exposed to so many messages about perfecting their appearance, they can come to think it's actually possible to do. And then they feel like failures if they don't match the images of unreal perfection that surround us every day.

We parents have a key role to play in opposing the messages about appearance that our daughters get. We need to teach them about their inner beauty and its value. When we help a girl value her unique beauty, we give her a priceless gift.

What to Say and Do

1–7 YEARS OLD

Tell her that she's beautiful when she's full of energy or radiating pride.

- You look beautiful when you're singing.

Describe all kinds of people as pretty and beautiful.

- You and Krissy are very different and you're both pretty.

8–13 YEARS OLD

Limit how much you comment on appearance. Focus instead on someone's character and actions.

- I want to be as interesting as Leonore when I'm old. She's always learning new things.
- Our new neighbors are so welcoming and warm. I like being around them.

Respond to her concerns and questions about her appearance with reassurance and perspective. She may focus on her appearance when the real issue is something deeper and harder to talk about.

- I know that going to a new school you want to feel as good as possible on the first day. Wearing clothes you feel comfortable in is part of that, but it's not the most important part.
- You're not happy with your hair today. I think there's probably something else going on, too. Any thoughts on what the other things are?

14 AND UP

Talk regularly about society's focus on appearance and how it can be harmful.

- It's really hard not to buy into all the messages about how you should look. I struggle with it, too.

- When I'm feeling tired, I worry more about how I look.

Notice when she expresses her true self in her appearance.

- When you wear that shirt, I know you're feeling good. It's you!

- You look so jazzy in purple. It suits you.

Words and Phrases to Use

- Inner beauty
- Authentic
- Accomplishment
- Talents
- Independent
- Original

- Unique
- Gorgeous
- Energetic
- Creative
- Beauty is in the eye of the beholder.

What Not to Say and Do

Don't judge your own or others' appearance. Don't say things like

- Ugh, I look awful today.
- She looks terrible. Doesn't she care?

Don't let it pass uncommented if she puts her own appearance down.

Don't buy into society's narrow definition of attractiveness.

Words and Phrases To Avoid

- Perfect

- Ugly

- Homely

- Average

- There are just a few truly beautiful people.

Resources

The Body Project by Joan Jacobs Brumberg. Vintage, 1998.

Real Gorgeous by Kaz Cooke. W.W. Norton, 1996.

You Have to Say I'm Pretty, You're My Mother: How to Help Your Daughter Learn to Love Her Body and Herself by Stephanie Pierson and Phyllis Cohen. Simon & Schuster, 2003.

Turn Beauty Inside Out Campaign: www.tbio.org

ASSERTIVENESS

"Tessa overheard me on the phone talking with a co-worker I was upset with the other day. When I got off, she asked why my voice had been higher-pitched and softer than usual. I wasn't aware of it but realized she was right. I'd changed my voice because I didn't want to sound rude and too emotional. But that downplayed the issue and in the end, my co-worker didn't take what I said seriously. How do I teach my daughter the difference between being rude and being assertive for good communication?"—Sylvia

Things to Consider

Assertiveness is being able to communicate what you need or want without attacking or blaming others. It's *not* selfishness or manipulation. Ideally, girls should develop and practice assertiveness *before* puberty as a counterweight to some of the changes that start to happen then. When a girl gets to puberty, she may often be confused about what she wants or needs. On top of that, she'll get messages from society that she should adapt her wants or needs to other people's expectations. If she already trusts her strong inner voice and has learned how to communicate assertively, she'll have the advantage of being in touch with her needs and wants. She's also had the experience of asking for what she wants and knowing she's not in control of the response. Being assertive doesn't mean always getting what she wants. It just means she has the confidence to ask for it directly. We can teach our daughters assertiveness by showing them how to identify their wants and needs and then how to express them to others.

We can teach her consideration for others and how to express her feelings and opinions honestly with courtesy and respect. But if any specific situation comes down to a choice between her voice and "being nice," we need to choose her voice and show her that we will back her up when she speaks up about something that's important. She needs to see that we value her voice as a key part of herself and we won't ever expect her to deny who she is in order to maintain her relationship with us. Having this bedrock in her relationship with us makes it possible for her to keep her strong voice in other relationships as she grows up.

What to Say and Do

1–7 YEARS OLD
Help her learn how to recognize her wants and needs and then talk about them.

- It looks like you want to go outside. Tell me that in words.

- You need something to eat? What would you like?

- You look sad. How do you feel? Do you need a hug?

Listen carefully and get to know her true voice as her sense of self develops.

8–13 YEARS OLD
Teach her to use a strong, steady voice (not the same as a loud voice) when asking for what she wants.

- I listen carefully when you use a strong voice.

- When you use a strong voice I know you really mean what you're saying.

- When you say something and then say, "I don't know" after it, I'm not sure how seriously to take it.

When she indicates she needs something but doesn't ask for it directly, help her do that.

- I'm getting the idea that you need something but I'm not sure what. Tell me about it.

- Respond directly when she makes a direct request. Even if you don't do what she wants, respond to her and praise her for asking.

- You explained what you want very clearly. I'm not going to give it to you because I think you're not old enough yet. I'm still glad you asked me.

Encourage her to be assertive with friends. Girls often feel they shouldn't have to ask friends for anything.

- Casey is a good friend but she can't read your mind. You need to tell her what you want. How could you say it?

Be aware of how you use your voice and model being authentic in matching your voice to your feelings.

Support her in figuring out how to be both honest and respectful of others at the same time.

14 AND UP

Give her positive feedback when she uses her authentic voice for both "positive" and "negative" things. Give her your full attention when she uses her true voice.

Support the importance of her awareness and expression of her needs and wants.

- Knowing what you want is the first step to maybe getting it.

- Your needs are a very important part of you.

If she's in a romantic relationship, support her assertiveness there.

- Being in love is wonderful. You both have your own wants and needs, and it's important that you both can speak up for them.

Words, Phrases, and Actions to Use

- Real

- Authentic

- True

- Self

- Speak up.

- Tell me what you need.

- You know what you want better than I do.

- Ask her to explain to you if you don't understand.

- You can always ask, and I'll think about it carefully.

- If you don't ask, the answer will always be no.

What Not to Say and Do

Don't contradict her when she tells you what she wants or needs. Don't say,

- You don't really want to do that. You just think you do.

- How could you possibly need to rest? You had a good night's sleep.

Don't give her what she wants if she's indirect about it. Don't say:

- I could tell how much you wanted it so I got it for you.

Words, Phrases, and Actions To Avoid

- Don't give in to whining.

- Don't ask.

- It's bad manners to ask.

- Don't be selfish.

Resources

Assertiveness by Kate Havelin. Capstone Press, 1999.

The Complete Idiot's Guide to Assertiveness by Jeff P. Davidson. Alpha, 1997.

Meeting at the Crossroads by Lyn Mikel Brown and Carol Gilligan. Random House, 1993.

BABYSITTING

"Leona is eleven and stays home by herself for up to two hours when we're not there in the afternoon and early evening. She's never done any babysitting but would like to start earning some of her own money. She's the youngest in our family. How do I know if she's ready for this responsibility? How do I help her be a good babysitter?"—Elaine

Things to Consider

Babysitting is a big step for girls and boys in developing responsibility. Sometimes we assume that girls are more natural babysitters than boys and will just know what to do by instinct. Other times, we can't imagine how our daughter could be old enough to take care of someone else's child. We worry about things that might happen that she wouldn't know how to handle. We're afraid that the child might get hurt accidentally while she's babysitting.

A girl who's prepared for babysitting and doing it for a child who's not too young (or too old) for her to take care of can gain valuable confidence and independence from the experience. Relying on her judgment and her persuasive abilities to care for a younger child makes her feel capable and powerful. Making decisions about what to do when a problem comes up gives her confidence for solving other problems. Earning her own money and negotiating a fair price to charge are important steps on the road to financial literacy. Our role is to make sure she's ready for the responsibility, knows what to do in an emergency, and has us as backup in the first year or two.

What to Say and Do

10 AND UP
Even if she's had extensive experience helping care for younger siblings or cousins, make sure she takes a babysitting class. (Many Red Cross branches and hospitals offer them.) The first aid training alone is crucial. Completing the class and getting the certificate show her commitment to babysitting. Arrange for her to help a parent out with care while the parent is still home so she can learn with supervision.

- The class will teach you things I might not know.

- Having the certificate will show parents that you'll be a good sitter and they'll trust you more.

- Tell me what they talked about in class today.

- I know you want to babysit on your own. And the Kims will do that after you spend a couple hours in charge of the kids while they're still home. It's like training wheels when you learned to ride a bike.

Have her first few jobs take place when one of her parents or one of the "customer" parents is totally available to answer questions on the phone or even help in person if need be.

- Call me with any questions.

- If you want, I can call you in about an hour to check in. (Only call if she wants you to.)

- If she calls with a question and it's not an emergency, say, "What do you think the babysitting teacher would say?"

When she gets home, ask her to tell you about the children she took care of. Listen for issues that arose and offer suggestions on what she could do if the situation happens again.

■ So Randy had trouble going to sleep? I wonder what his parents do for his bedtime routine?

Words and Phrases to Use

■ Responsible	■ Listen
■ Problem solver	■ Job
■ Good ideas	■ Worker
■ Fun	

What Not to Say and Do

Don't hover and transfer to her your anxiety about her first few babysitting jobs. If she's not well prepared enough, help her gain more skills before her first job. Don't say,

■ Here's a list of all the things you'll probably forget.

Don't act like her job is unimportant. Don't say,

■ I'd rather take you shopping this morning. Just call the Steins and tell them you can't come.

■ It doesn't matter what they pay you. Taking care of kids isn't really work.

Don't let her take a friend along unless she's very experienced and you know the friend won't distract her from her focus on the children.

Resources

The Babysitter's Handbook by Harriet N. Brown. Pleasant Company Publications, 1999.

American Red Cross: www.redcross.org

Online Babysitter Class: www.forgirlsandtheirdreams.org

BODY IMAGE

While body image may not seem to be an issue until a girl reaches puberty and her body starts changing, it's crucial to build a strong foundation of positive body image for your daughter before that time. How she feels about her body is a key part of a girl's sense of who she is as she gets older.

1–7 YEARS OLD

Four-year-old Grace and her dad are visiting relatives who don't see Grace very often and want to compliment her. One calls her "a heart stealer" and warns Dad he'll have to "watch out for those boys," while another comments on her "cute figure" and how lucky it is Grace "didn't get the family thunder thighs." Grace looks down at the floor, embarrassed, and tries to hide behind Dad. Dad feels vaguely uncomfortable but doesn't know quite why or how to respond.

8–13 YEARS OLD

Eleven-year-old Katie is of normal height and weight, and she's started adding noticeable body fat as her body changes from girl to woman. When shopping for a bathing suit, Katie is obviously miserable, even though her mom Jana thinks she looks cute in every suit and tells her so. Jana is mystified at Katie's reaction, since clothes shopping has always been one of their favorite activities. Back home, Katie's dad Peter asks to see the new suit. Katie says nothing and storms off to her room. Peter says, "What did I do?"

"It was a disaster," Jana replies.

14 AND UP

Keisha tries on a strapless style when shopping for a prom dress. She's small breasted and the bodice is loose. As soon as her mom Susan suggests a different dress, Keisha gets upset, asking, "Why am I so flat? I need a Wonderbra."

Shocked, Susan says, "You're barely fifteen. No daughter of mine is going to look like a call girl."

Things to Consider

Girls face huge pressures about body image starting at a very young age. At puberty, even more pressures hit just as a girl's body starts to naturally change and add fat. Bombarded with unrealistic, "perfect" images in movies, TV, and advertising, almost every girl has serious trouble feeling good, or even OK, about her body.

Plastic surgery among teen girls increased alarmingly in the past five years, a sign that parents are allowing and encouraging it. Girls with physical disabilities face additional body-image struggles and discrimination or ostracizing for how they look. No wonder problems with body image are appearing at younger and younger ages.

Every girl needs to know her own strengths, the goodness of how her body works, and the ways it helps her fulfill her dreams. Feeling good about her body is a great boost to her confidence. Parents and other significant adults in a girl's life have the greatest influence on her body image. You can help your girl develop and maintain a strong body image no matter what her natural body shape is, and you can help her fight the inevitable struggles every girl has with her body. Both moms and dads have special roles to play: Mom in how she relates to and talks about her own body, and Dad in how he talks about women's and girls' bodies (not as sex objects). Both parents must confront and oppose the presentation of girls and women as sex objects, explaining why it's harmful.

What to Say and Do

1–7 YEARS OLD

Regularly praise your own body and your daughter's body for what it does, not how it looks.

- You are so strong.

- You can kick the soccer ball very straight.

Reassure her that she is uniquely beautiful. Sincerely praise things she might see as imperfections.

- I love that birthmark on your shoulder.

- Your frizzy hair is so full of energy!

Help her learn to use her body in sports or dance or play, getting joy from its capabilities.

- You sure love to ride your bike.

- Can you teach me that new tae kwon do kick?

8–13 YEARS

Notice when she feels good about her body, create more of those experiences, and remind her of them.

- Look at this picture of you dancing when you were little. You look so happy.

- Your whole body concentrates when you're playing the drums.

Encourage conversation about irrational body-image messages, even making fun of them.

- It sure would be great if being taller would solve all our problems!

- It's ridiculous to see such perfect airbrushed photos in magazines. They look so fake.

14 AND UP

Help her identify contradictions and harmful stereotypes about body image.

- Isn't it strange that fat people are automatically assumed to be lazy?

- Do you think large-breasted women are happier than small-breasted ones?

Encourage her to be active in any activity where her body's usefulness is not determined by how it looks.

Comment regularly about body shape being determined by genetics. If she's not your biological daughter, take that into consideration.

- Look how much alike you and I were at eight years old.

- I have a round belly just like my mom and Granny.

Let her express her frustrations about body image by listening more than you comment.

- Tell me what bugs you about that.

If anyone makes negative or sexual comments about her body, say, "I don't want you to talk about my daughter like that."

Words and Phrases to Use

- Strong

- It runs in our family.

- I love your . . .

What Not to Say and Do

Don't make negative comments about anyone's body, especially your own or hers.

- Look how his arm is jiggling. Gross!
- If only I had a smaller waist I'd feel prettier.

Don't ignore it when she feels insecure about her body. Don't say,

- Don't worry about it.
- You'll grow out of it.

Just offering clichés, without backing them up by your own actions, won't help her feel good. If you say the following, show that you believe it.

- Looks aren't really important.

- All that matters is what's inside.

Don't avoid talking about body image. She might think there's something wrong with her.

Don't make sexually suggestive comments about her body, even if you think they're compliments.

Resources

101 Ways to Help Your Daughter Love Her Body by Brenda Richardson and Elaine Rehr. HarperCollins, 2001.

200 Ways to Love the Body You Have by Marcia Germaine Hutchinson. Crossing Press, 1999.

Body Wars: Making Peace with Women's Bodies by Margo Maine. Gurze Books, 2000.

Bodylove: Learning to Like Our Looks and Ourselves by Rita Freedman. Gurze Books, 2002.

Turn Beauty Inside Out Campaign: www.tbio.org

BOUNDARIES

"My daughter Rosa was independent and didn't care what others thought of her as a preschooler. Now in fourth grade, it seems like she's stopped thinking for herself. She changes her clothes, hobbies, actions, and words to follow her classmates even when I'm sure she thinks otherwise. At home she tries to fix how everyone else in the family is feeling."—Simon

Things to Consider

As a girl grows up, she becomes less and less dependent on her parents and grows steadily into her own, individual person, with unique perspectives and wants. She needs to develop healthy boundaries to keep herself physically, emotionally, and psychologically healthy. Girls are taught in many subtle ways to place the greatest importance on maintaining relationships with others, even if that means doing some things that don't feel right or violate her values. Particularly in preadolescence and early adolescence, girls need parental support to stay true to themselves and not lose sight of themselves in the fads and behaviors of some of their peers. We want to teach a girl how to keep a healthy balance between her own deepest needs and the needs and feelings of others.

The tug-of-war between being her authentic self and becoming the person others want her to be is key in a girl's development. The more we affirm our daughter's true self and teach her how to respect and protect herself with healthy boundaries, the less effect the tug-of-war will have, particularly in adolescence.

What to Say and Do

1–7 YEARS OLD
Encourage her to recognize and exercise her own likes and dislikes in as many ways as feasible, especially when different from yours.

- You want peanut butter instead of egg salad even though I like the opposite. Great!

- Those polka dots and stripes together give you your own special look.

Let her say yes and no freely when it comes from her heart, and try to understand what it's about even if you need to tell her you won't do what she wants.

- It's OK to say, "No thank you," when you don't feel good about doing something.

- I understand you don't want to hold my hand crossing the street because you feel grown up, but I need to do that.

8–13 YEARS OLD
Encourage her to listen to her own inner voice, and talk with her about her feelings and beliefs, especially when she's feeling conflict.

- How do you feel about Chaundra saying that about Becky?

- What feels right to you?

Support her when she takes a stand and when she negotiates a compromise between her needs and the needs of others.

- I like the way you told your little sister that you needed to be alone for a while after school and would read to her after dinner.

- It sounds like it was hard to tell Ms. Rubin that you think it's wrong to kill a frog to dissect it. I'm proud that you told her why you feel that way.

14 AND UP

Create healthy boundaries for her when she isn't doing it for herself.

- You can go to the movies with several friends, including Aaron, but not just the two of you. I'll be able to give you all a ride.

- I'll call Elly's dad to make sure he'll be there during the party.

- Our rule is only two kids in the car when the driver is under eighteen.

Give her practice in being assertive with peers or friends when she doesn't want to do something they ask.

- What would you say to Teri if she asked you to tell her mom she was over here when she was really meeting her boyfriend behind her mom's back?

- How would you decide what to do if you and Jenny were at the mall with kids from school and they started to put things from a store in their purses?

Words and Phrases to Use

- What feels right to you?

- What do you want to do?

- How do you feel?

- You know yourself.

What Not to Say and Do

Don't give her the message that she's responsible for meeting your emotional needs. Don't say,

- You only think of yourself. You never think of how you can help me.

Don't guilt her for respectfully having a different opinion or feelings from you or others.

- How could you think that?

- You don't really think that's important, do you?

- Why can't you just be agreeable?

Resources

Boundaries by Anne Katherine. Fireside, 1993.

Peer Pressure Reversal: An Adult Guide to Developing a Responsible Child by Sharon Scott. Human Resource Development, 1997.

BOYS

"My younger daughter Steph is nine and is sometimes downright mean to some of the boys in the neighborhood. 'All boys are dumb' has become her constant refrain. On the other hand, my fifteen-year-old Ariel has a nice bunch of friends from church, boys and girls, but she spends so much time with them that I'm afraid a serious romance will break out, and she's just not ready for that."—Marie

Things to Consider

Girls tend to develop faster than boys intellectually, emotionally, and sometimes physically in the preadolescent and early adolescent years. So it's not unusual for a nine-year-old to be bossy, impatient, and even rude with male peers who may not yet have the same skills she has.

By middle school and high school, girls are much more interested in spending time with boys. This desire is not always romantic or sexual. Teen girls and boys really can be just good friends! However, our culture is awash in sexual innuendo (even about children), and there's often a de facto assumption that any girl-boy pair must be romantic, or about to become romantic. Don't get caught in that trap; focus on how your daughter is emerging into a whole person, not just a sexual one.

What to Say and Do

1–7 YEARS OLD

Encourage her to play with girl and boy peers and relatives. Encourage her to see peers and adults as people before she sees them as a gender and to understand that everyone has different abilities.

- You're frustrated that Jim can't read as fast as you. But teasing makes it harder for him to learn. What can you do instead?

- Your cousins Shaniqua and Sean are coming for the weekend. What will all three of you enjoy doing together?

8–13 YEARS OLD

Encourage her to value herself and her friends (female or male) for what they do and think, not for their romantic potential. Let her know it's normal and okay to like a boy in a nonromantic way.

- I liked the way you and Hank were neck and neck at soccer today. You really challenge each other, and it makes you both better players.

- Church camp was great when I was a kid because no one there seemed too interested in boyfriend-girlfriend stuff. We were able to be just friends. Patty and Josef are still my friends today.

- It was really fun to listen to you and the gang talking about the movie and getting excited about its ideas.

14 AND UP

See her as more than just a vulnerable sexual being (I'm talking to you, Dad). Continue to focus on all of her qualities, and do the same with her friends.

- It's neat the way you and Sergio talk about your favorite books.

- That was a tough thing to tell Andre and Rachel. You handled it really well, and so did they. I admire how honest you three are with each other.

- Want to invite the gang over for a picnic on Saturday?

Make sure others respect her relationships, too.

- Uncle Jeff, I don't like it when you tease Jessie about her friend Angelo. They are good friends, and it's disrespectful to assume that they're "an item" when she tells you they aren't.

Actions to Use

- Make time and space for girl and boy friends to be together at your house or other places.
- Mom, tell her stories about your adolescent friendships with boys.
- Let her see your good example in how you talk and work with adults of the other gender.

What Not to Say and Do

Don't give her the idea that girls and boys can only be romantically involved and not just regular friends.

Don't ignore her interests, abilities, and desires regarding boys.

Don't show prejudice against boys. Don't say,

- You shouldn't be interested in boys yet.
- Don't ever trust boys.

Don't refer to her male friend as "just" a friend.

Words and Phrases to Avoid

- Oooh, Kalisha has a boyfriend! (said in a teasing way)
- Who are you going to marry?

- You're not just friends. You can't fool me.

- Men and women can never be "just good friends," and neither can boys and girls.

Resources

Boy v. Girl? How Gender Shapes Who We Are, What We Want, and How We Get Along by George Abrahams, PhD, and Sheila Ahlbrand. Free Spirit Publishing, 2002.

CHANGE

"My five-year-old Javonne likes to know what's going to happen before it happens. When things don't go the way she expects them to, she gets upset. I can understand how she feels, but I'm concerned that this is going to be a problem for her when she gets older. How can I help her understand that change is part of life and that she can adapt to it and maybe even enjoy it?"—Malika

Things to Consider

We've heard the saying, "Change is the only constant," and our own lives are examples of its truth. We can see that people who accept change and "roll with it" seem to have an easier time in life, and we'd like to help our daughters take that approach. This can be easier said than done.

It helps to remember that children's lives are usually out of their control and influenced by changes that they don't see or understand, let alone feel they can influence. Seen from this perspective, many girls are better at coping with change than we give them credit for. Some girls will take major changes in stride, and others will find even small changes challenging. Adapt your response to the individual girl.

There are things we can do to help our daughters accept change and see that it can often be positive. The most basic thing is to provide a stable daily environment as much as possible. Toddlers and preschoolers rely on adults for predictable structure in mealtime, nap time, playtime, bedtime, and so on. Even when she's older, a reliable daily routine will provide a strong foundation that helps her cope with unexpected change. It can also help to talk with her ahead of time about change that you know is coming up. Explain the possibilities, encourage her to express her feelings about them, and then prompt her to think through choices in how she will respond to the change. During her adolescence, share changes you are coping with so she can hear your thinking about them as well as see how you cope (or don't) with specific situations. This also lets her see that sometimes even changes we resist can be positive in the long run.

What to Say and Do

1–7 YEARS OLD
Acknowledge the lack of control she may feel about changes.

- I know it's hard to stop playing when it's time to go home.

- Sometimes I wish things could just stay the way they are.

Reinforce and help her express positive feelings about change.

- I'm glad you like the new teacher even though you miss Mark.

- I know you were sad about giving your tricycle to Laila. It was very kind and grown up of you.

8–13 YEARS OLD
Acknowledge that change in self and relationships can be both liberating and difficult in these years.

- You feel like you've changed and Janey hasn't.

- You're asking more questions in class than you were last year.

Invite her to both remember and imagine positive change.

- If you were president, what would you change?

- I remember when you felt scared of the dark.

- I'm going to miss our neighbors when we move. But I'm so excited about my new job!

14 AND UP

Help her explore what she wants to change and what she needs to accept.

- Let's see what you can do about that.

- It sounds like that's just the way it is right now.

Share and discuss changes in your life.

- I don't like how Miriam only talks about herself, so I'm spending less time with her.

- My new boss expects a lot more of me. It's scary, but I'm doing it.

Words and Phrases to Use

- What do you think will happen?

- Could it be better?

- What can we do?

- Different

What Not to Say and Do

Avoid negative speculation about the future. It can make her apprehensive and nervous.

- I won't be able to stand it if that happens.

- That will never work.

Don't encourage her to think that things she can't control are always negative.

- Why do things always happen to me?

Describe change without making a comparison.

Words and Phrases to Avoid

- It was so much better before.
- Control
- Better

- Worse
- Forever
- Always

Resources

When You're Falling, Dive by Cheri Huber. Keep It Simple Books, 2003.

CHORES

"My daughter Lani complains about every chore we give her. She procrastinates and whines and doesn't do it well. It's a lot easier to just do it myself. Why does she make such a big deal about it?"—Zach

Things to Consider

Chores are good for girls. They learn how to handle responsibility, they learn useful skills, and they have the satisfaction of accomplishment and contributing to the family. When girls complain and sabotage chores, there is likely something else behind it. Is she being given chores that are too advanced for her age, or too many chores at once? Are chores the battleground in a power struggle between you and her? Are chores handed out unfairly in your family (girls do all housework and boys do all outdoor work)? Are you inconsistent in giving her a chore and then finishing it when she doesn't? Are you overly critical of how she does chores, making it virtually impossible for her to satisfy you? Take a look at the overall situation and decide what the problem really is, and then you'll know how to approach it.

What to Say and Do

1–7 YEARS OLD

Give her chores that are small and can be completed in five to ten minutes. Show her how to do them.

Give her a lot of leeway in doing a chore her way as long as it gets done.

- You put all your socks in the drawer! Very good.

- You picked up all your toys before dinner. Thanks!

8–13 YEARS OLD

If chores become a power struggle, address that directly.

- I don't think this is about the chores. I think it's about who's in charge.

Give her more complicated chores as she's able to do them.

Be sparing in criticism of how she does chores as long as they are done reasonably well. Perfection is an impossible standard for her to meet.

Give positive feedback when she does something well.

- You did a great job cutting the lawn. It looks professional!

Communicate clearly about the consequences for undone chores.

- This needs to be done before 8 p.m. tonight. If it's not done, you'll lose a privilege this weekend.

Give her some choices and variety of chores if she'd like that.

- Here's the list of chores for this week. You can pick the five you want to do.

14 AND UP

Teens actually have trouble remembering to do chores. Talk about a way for her to remember with notes or a chart.

- You have a lot on your mind. Let's try a chart for the chores so they're all right there. You check each off when it's done and I won't need to ask.

- I'm frustrated with your chores being undone. I don't want to nag anymore. What do you suggest as a solution?

Words and Phrases to Use

- Pitch in.
- It's your chore.
- You can do it your way.

- Well done.
- Good job.
- Thanks for your help.

What Not to Say and Do

Don't take over on her chores. Don't say,

- You're doing it wrong. Let me do it.
- It's easier to do it myself!
- I already did it. I knew you'd just whine.

Don't blame or guilt her. Don't say,

- You never remember anything.
- You don't care about me at all.
- It's your fault. You did it wrong.
- You can't do anything right.

Resources

Rewards for Kids: Charts and Activities for Positive Parenting by Virginia M. Schiller. American Psychological Association, 2003.

CITIZENSHIP

"After the last election I was shocked to find out how many people I know didn't vote. It seems to be especially true of young people in their twenties and thirties. Of course, my daughter Selena can't vote yet, but how do I make sure she grows up to be a responsible citizen?"—Nadine

Things to Consider

It can be challenging to get your girl interested in something as abstract as voting when she won't be able to do it until she's eighteen. It's important to find ways to give kids a chance to vote unofficially (through kids' voting projects), and it's also crucial that you bring your kids to the polls with you when you vote. Sometimes kids' curiosity even motivates parents to vote!

As important as voting is, it's only part of being an involved citizen. Nearly every other aspect of citizenship is open to girls at various ages. Broaden your daughter's understanding of citizenship to include volunteering, making charitable donations, learning about community or political issues, reading the newspaper, writing a letter to the editor, e-mailing her member of congress, running for a school or club office, not littering, and respecting other people. With a definition like this, a girl can feel that her citizenship makes a difference every day in ways big and small, and that's what it's all about.

What to Say and Do

1–7 YEARS OLD

Give her the awareness that she's part of the community beyond your family, bringing her along, if possible, when you do community activities. Take her with you to vote.

- Come help me shovel Mr. Smith's walk. He can't do it because of his broken ankle.

- What food do we want to give to the food shelf? Help me pick out three things.

8–13 YEARS OLD

Respond to her interest in specific issues like stray animals, homelessness, the environment, racism, girls' rights, and poverty. Help her find ways to do something about the issues she cares about.

- That's very upsetting. What do you think you can do to help?

- Do you want to write to Senator Snowe about it?

- Here's the phone number for the town's animal shelter. I bet they need volunteers.

Encourage her to develop and explain her opinions on community issues and also to respect views that are different from hers. Show her how you do that.

- I'm glad you have an opinion. I'm interested to hear how you came to it.

- I disagree with Grandpa on whom to vote for, but we talked about it and now I understand some of his reasons.

14 AND UP

Gently challenge her reasoning to help her strengthen confidence in her opinions.

- Tell me why you think that. I'm not sure I agree.

- Is there any research on the Internet about that? I'd like to learn more.

Stress the importance of taking action (including supporting others) on the issues she cares about.

- Are you going to run for class president since you think the hall rules are dumb?

- Sexist jokes bug me. I never laugh at them and I try to calmly say, "That upsets me."

Words and Phrases to Use

- What do you think?

- I never thought of it that way before.

- I'm listening.

- Good point.

- Actions speak as loud as words.

- Always vote.

- Here's something we can do about it.

What Not to Say and Do

Don't let others belittle her opinions because she's young, and don't do it yourself. Don't say,

- What do you know?

- You're just a little kid.

- Who cares?

Don't act like no one can change community problems. Don't treat all politicians with disdain. Don't say,

- Of course he's a crook. He's a politician.

- It's too big to do anything about.

Words and Phrases to Avoid

- What does it matter?

- No one cares.

- Impossible

- What an idiot.

- Who do you think you are?

Resources

Kid's Guide to Social Action by Barbara A. Lewis. Free Spirit Publishing, 1998.

The White House Project: www.thewhitehouseproject.org

Take Action: A Guide to Active Citizenship by Marc Kielburger. John Wiley & Sons, 2002.

CLIQUES

"My thirteen-year-old daughter has been through several groups of girl-friends and has yet to find someone she can trust. She has one best friend from outside of school but continues to have problems with the girls at her school."—Celeste

Things to Consider

Cliques have been part of middle school for a long time, but lately this type of behavior seems to be occurring even younger. It's natural for girls to want to find a group of friends they feel comfortable with, especially as they want to depend more on friends for support during adolescence. But cliques are groups based on exclusion, not support. They are defined by who's "in" and who's "out," definitions that change mysteriously and often. Being "in" one week is no guarantee of belonging the next week.

Cliques are part of relational aggression, meaning the use of relationships to hurt others. It's more subtle than physical violence and includes gossip, exclusion, and teasing. Girls are more likely than boys to use relationships to hurt others. Awareness of and direct communication with your daughter about these issues is crucial even if she doesn't bring it up to you. She might feel too ashamed to talk about it if she's "out" and could be hurting others if she's "in."

What to Say and Do

1–7 YEARS OLD

Realize cliquey behavior can show up at this age, although it's less common. Talking directly with other parents about stopping it is appropriate. Teach your daughter to have empathy for others.

- It sounds like you were feeling left out. Tell me about it.

- It was kind of you to ask Shauna if she felt angry when she walked away at recess.

8–13 YEARS OLD

Involve her in nonschool groups that are based on her interests and developing her skills, not on popularity. Feeling capable and confident reduces the likelihood she'll join a clique.

- You have a real talent for that.

- The group needs your creative thinking.

Admit that cliques are a reality and prepare her to resist cliquey behavior directed at others.

- What would you do if Charmay sent you an IM saying Olivia was weird?

- When Kellie acts like that, it's because she feels insecure. What could you do?

Ask questions and listen closely if you suspect she's part of a clique. Tell her why that's not OK.

- I heard you and Jessica talking about "the geeky kids," and I felt uncomfortable about what you both said. It sounds like you were making fun of them.

- Cliques hurt other people and they don't help you.

14 AND UP

Help her develop strategies and role-play how to handle it if she's targeted by a clique.

- What would you do if a rumor started about you?

Support her in being empathetic and doing what is right. Understand that it can be difficult.

- Your loyalty and friendship to Mandy is so important to her.

- I'm proud you're brave enough to be kind to the unpopular kids.

Words and Phrases to Use

- Kindness
- Understanding
- Insecurity
- Strong
- Feelings

- Do what's right.
- The golden rule
- Individuality
- Differences

What Not to Say and Do

Don't encourage her to accept behavior or treat others in ways she doesn't want to be treated. Don't say,

- Sometimes you have to just go along. That's how groups are.
- She was mean to you, so you should be mean back.

Don't ignore signs that she might be part of a clique. Don't say,

- She's just making a big deal out of nothing.
- She's a tattletale if she runs to the teacher about that.

Resources

Cliques by Charlene C. Gianetti and Margaret Sagarese. Broadway Books, 2001.

Girl Wars: 12 Strategies That Will End Female Bullying by Cheryl Dellasega and Charisse Nixon. Fireside, 2003.

Girlfighting: Betrayal and Rejection Among Girls by Lyn Mikel Brown. New York University Press, 2003.

Odd Girl Out by Rachel Simmons. Harcourt, 2002.

Queen Bees and Wannabees by Rosalind Wiseman. Crown Publishing, 2002.

CLOTHES, HAIR, AND MAKEUP

"Clothing, hairstyle, and makeup were a battleground between me and my mother, and I don't want it to be the same for me and Eliza. But the popular clothes she wants are too sexy and expensive, and the hairstyles and makeup some girls her age wear make them look twenty-five. What can I do?"—Bev

Things to Consider

Clothing, hair, and makeup become battlegrounds because girls know that how they look is a way to fit in or stand out. Parents often feel that a daughter's choices reflect on them and that they need to keep her from making embarrassing mistakes.

But most experts agree that such "mistakes" are truly harmless and should be ignored. When you treat these things with a light touch, your approach gives her a strong message that who she is matters much more than how she looks. The example Mom sets is crucial. If Mom feels comfortable with her own personal style, whatever it is, that does two things. It shows your daughter that you can be yourself and have fun with clothing, hair, and makeup, and it reduces parents' anxiety about girls experimenting with their looks. That's a message every girl needs to counter the massive amounts of advertising and media coverage, which make these things seem much more important than they are.

Starting early, you can help your daughter chart a path of making her own choices, while understanding that she will probably go along with the crowd, at least part of the time. That's not a failure; it's actually part of developing her individuality.

What to Say and Do

1–7 YEARS OLD

Let her dress and wear her hair the way she wants as much as possible. Notice how her choices express her personality. Don't think of it as a reflection on you.

- What do you want to wear? Good choice.

- That shirt is a beautiful color. I think of you whenever I see that color.

- You cut your own hair. Good for you!

8–13 YEARS OLD

Understand she'll probably do more "going along" with trends at this age. She may want to appear older than she is as a way of feeling grown up. It will be a shorter phase if you don't turn it into a fight and you gently help her get perspective on how quickly and irrationally styles change.

- That seems to be what everyone's wearing right now. What do you think will be the fad in six months?

- If you want to dye your hair when you're twelve, you can try it then.

Comment casually on your own and other people's choices to buck the trends.

- I'm glad that style changed; I never liked it and I didn't wear it.

- I've noticed that Jasmine always puts her hair in a ponytail.

Give her a monthly clothing/hair budget to provide limits on what you'll spend.

- You can get that. Then you'll have fifteen dollars for the rest of the month.

Provide clear limits and explanations if certain clothing/hair/makeup choices are out of bounds with your values.

- I'm not OK with those tight, short skirts. They're hard to sit in and they are too revealing.

- You can try on makeup at home, but you'll have to wait until you're thirteen to wear it to school.

14 AND UP

Accept that she'll make her own choices now and give support when she dresses in her personal style. Remember that clothes, hair, and makeup are impermanent, will probably change, and can be a way to have fun together.

- You look so comfortable in that.

- I'm surprised, but I like your hair that color.

- Can you come shopping and help me pick out something new for my birthday?

Words and Phrases to Use

- Comfort

- Quality

- Your style

- Personality

- Playful

What Not to Say and Do

Don't overemphasize clothes, hair, and makeup. Don't pressure her to dress the way you do. Don't say,

- Clothes make the person.

- What will people think if you wear that?

- The way you look reflects on me.

Don't expect her to never follow a trend. Don't say,

- You're just a follower.

- If Laronna jumped off a cliff, would you?

Words and Phrases to Avoid

- What did you do to your hair?

- Why are you wearing that?

COMPETITION

"Ayala avoids direct competition. She doesn't play competitive sports or like to compete for grades or attention. Generally this is fine. But every now and then I think a little bit of competitive spirit would be good for her." —Jeff

Things to Consider

Some girls are genuinely noncompetitive, but that's unusual. More often they compete in indirect ways that they don't think of as competition. Girls often get the message that direct competition is unfeminine, associated with people's feelings getting hurt. They see adult women competing indirectly through popularity, appearance, clothing, housekeeping, marriage, and their children. So they learn to submerge their competitive feelings, but the irony is that indirect competition leads to hurt feelings much more than open competition.

Overcompetitiveness can be unhealthy and make her unhappy. But many girls will benefit from being allowed to be consciously and openly competitive in appropriate situations. This is an opportunity to offer them some external feedback on their performance and help them see ways to improve. And conscious, open competition will reduce her tendency to be indirectly competitive, which is more likely to harm her and others.

What to Say and Do

1–7 YEARS OLD
Recognize her competitive feelings and identify them nonjudgmentally.

- You like to win when we play cards.

- You like to be in the front of the line.

- You feel good when people pick your idea.

8 AND UP
Provide structured situations where there is healthy, open competition.

- This Scottish dancing group holds competitions. Let's check it out.

- I like to see you doing some things that include competition. It stretches you.

Let her experience losing. Empathize with the disappointment. Help her learn from losing.

- When your penalty kick missed the goal, it was so disappointing. I'm glad the coach didn't blame you and gave you some tips for practicing a different way.

Mention it when you see her competing indirectly.

- I noticed that you and Mary were competing in talking about how many friends you each have.

- Indirect competition hurts feelings because it's pretending not to be competitive when it really is.

Words and Phrases to Use

- Healthy competition
- Up to the challenge
- Finding a better way
- Improving

- Friendly competition
- Good sport
- Learn from competition.

What Not to Say and Do

Don't model indirect competition. Don't say,

- I just think our house is nicer than the Jackson's house.
- At least my clothes fit properly.
- There were more people at your party than at hers.

Don't tell her all competition is bad. Don't say,

- Never compete with a friend; it will end the friendship.
- Girls don't compete.
- It's not nice.

Resources

See Jane Win: The Rimm Report on How 1,000 Girls Became Successful Women by Sylvia Rimm, Sara Rimm-Kauffman, and Ilonna Jane Rimm. Running Press, 2001.

COMPLAINING

"I'm tired of Sidney complaining all the time. It seems like nothing's ever right, to hear her tell it. I usually just try to ignore the whining, but it gets on my nerves and sometimes I lose my patience. She has a pretty good life but doesn't seem to appreciate it. Is there something wrong with her, or am I doing something wrong?" —Latrice

Things to Consider

When girls complain, it's often labeled as whining and judged unimportant. It certainly may be whining about something minor (and if we're honest, we realize we do that, too). But don't automatically dismiss her complaints without listening to the substance of them. Even the most privileged young girls are relatively powerless in daily life, and their feeling of powerlessness can come out through complaints.

When you listen to your daughter's complaints and empathize with her powerlessness, it helps her feel understood, which helps her to accept things she can't change and also decide to change things she can. As she gets older and has more power in her life, complaints can be a kind of shorthand for expressing emotions like anger, fear, or anxiety that "go underground" in early adolescence.

How do you know when to take her complaints seriously? Listen carefully, notice if they seem different than usual, and ask probing questions to let her give you more specifics. Try to remember your deepest feelings and concerns at her age and think about what her complaint might be expressing. Though they may seem minor to us, remember that the challenges and problems she faces are very important to her. Her complaints may also be rooted in societal unfairness based on gender, race, religion, or economic status. When that's the case, it's most important to listen fully and then help her figure out what you can do together (often working with others outside your family) to change what's unfair.

What to Say and Do

1–7 YEARS OLD
Accept her complaints and let her express them. Help her understand that complaints can often be resolved. After listening, help her think through a solution.

- It seems like you're having trouble with that.

- Now that you've let that out, do we need to do something about it?

8–13 YEARS OLD
Admit that things aren't always fair. Help her decide when and how to be proactive and assertive about things that aren't fair. Also help her let go of things she really can't do anything about.

- You're right, that's not fair.

- What can we do to make it better?

- Since you can't change the situation, what do you want to do?

Help her explore the feelings underneath her complaints. Accept her feelings as reasonable even when you might feel they are about something minor. Your acceptance will help her process and let go of the complaint.

- Tell me more about that and why it bothers you.

- I understand where you're coming from.

14 AND UP

Use her complaints as a way to empower her to solve her own problems as much as possible. Encourage her to share her complaints with others as a way to put them in perspective and to brainstorm solutions.

- That sounds awful. What do you want to do?

- That's a tough problem. I wonder what Casey thinks?

Notice how much you complain and what you do about your own complaints.

Words and Phrases to Use

- Frustrating

- Understand

- Solution

- Make changes

- Brainstorm

What Not to Say and Do

Don't dismiss her complaints offhandedly. Don't say,

- Stop whining.

- You have nothing to complain about.

Don't belittle the things that concern her. Don't say,

- That's so petty.

- It's not the end of the world, now, is it?

Words and Phrases to Avoid

- Life's not fair.

- I don't want to hear about it.

- You're just whining.

- Forget about it.

- You're so ungrateful.

Resources

Stop Smiling, Start Kvetching: A 5-Step Guide to Creative Complaining by Barbara Held. St. Martin's Press, 2001.

COMPLIMENTS AND ENCOURAGEMENT

"I praise my teenagers regularly, and my son seems to revel in the encouragement. But when I applaud my two daughters, it often seems counterproductive: they go silent or get full of themselves or brush off the praise or get annoyed with me. Should I stifle my compliments?"—Harriette

Things to Consider

Girls learn contradictory expectations for themselves in our culture. On the one hand, they are encouraged to go for their dreams and accomplish ambitious goals. On the other hand, they are encouraged to put others first, be self-effacing, and not draw attention to their achievements. We don't want to raise obnoxious, conceited daughters, but we do want them to feel good about what they can do. It's important to consider two ideas:

As they get older, girls need more specific feedback in the praise they get. Dads may tend to be better at this than moms. As one fifteen-year-old girl told me, "After my soccer games, Mom is always like, 'Great job, honey!' and while that's fine, it doesn't mean much after a while. Dad usually goes something like, 'I liked the way you defended that rush at the start of the second half. Later on, it seemed like you and Cathy miscommunicated about who was covering whom. Did you notice that?' Sure, I'm not always crazy about hearing the bad, but being specific helps me get better at soccer, which is what I want."

Girls need to be empathetic, but not self-denying. It's important to compliment and encourage our daughters for what they do and think, especially when they're bombarded daily with the idea that how they look is more important than who they are. They need encouragement both when things seem difficult and when they seem to be going well. But we must also teach our kids—girls and boys—to care about those less fortunate than we, and to weigh how our actions will impact others. Girl power can be very powerful without tearing others down. Specificity in encouragement discourages a swelled head.

What to Say and Do

1–7 YEARS OLD

Encourage her to accomplish things that involve thinking, doing, pretending, and caring for others. General, overall praise is appropriate at younger ages.

- I love the way you love to run around the yard.

- I admire the way you helped your sister, even though you were tired.

- You have such a great imagination!

- You are beautiful when you stand up for yourself.

8–13 YEARS OLD

This is when girls start to need more specific and detailed compliments.

- It was great the way you worked out that conflict with Annie and didn't sell yourself short. What made you think of the approach you took?

- Your dribbling is improving a lot. Do you want to work with me on learning some behind-the-back moves?

- I read your story, and I really liked this part because the feelings and descriptions were so vivid. I had some trouble understanding this other part, though, so can you explain it to me?

14 AND UP

Situations, relationships, and accomplishments are getting more complex and nuanced. Your encouragement has to be that way, too.

- I know you feel discouraged about this science project, but I think you are on the right track and close to getting over the hump. Can I or someone else help you plan how to finish?

- Your recital was beautiful. I particularly liked the way you and Jamal seemed so in synch during the adagio. It made me smile big because you worked so hard on that section!

Actions to Use

- Give specific constructive feedback about her accomplishments and thoughts.

- Ask her if she wants to hear your feedback now or at a later time.

- Listen nonjudgmentally to her as she works out problems without jumping in to solve them for her. Then compliment her ability to figure out what she wants to do.

What Not to Say and Do

Don't undermine your encouragement with insincerity or the idea that you must always "balance" praise with criticism.

- That was good. What would you do better next time?

- Do you really think *that's* the way to do it?

- You did that pretty well, but you messed up at the end. What's wrong with you?

Actions to Avoid

- Don't attempt to "encourage" her by tearing her down.

- Avoid telling her that what she wants is always more important than what anyone else wants.

- Also avoid telling her that what anyone else wants is always more important than what she wants.

- Never offer overdoses of general, nonspecific praise.

Resources

200 Ways to Raise a Girl's Self-Esteem by Will Glennon. Red Wheel/Weiser, 1999.

Dads and Daughters: How to Inspire, Understand, and Support Your Daughter by Joe Kelly. Broadway Books, 2002.

Raising a Girl by Don and Jeanne Elium. Ten Speed Press, 2003.

COURAGE

"My eleven-year-old daughter seems fearless and willing to try anything. But my fourteen-year-old seems downright mousey. She never stands up for herself and won't even ride a roller coaster anymore."—Tabitha

Things to Consider

Before adolescence, girls are often quite bold and sassy, both bodily and psychologically. They are physically adventurous and daring, willing to try new things and get their clothes dirty. They speak right up with their opinions, even when that strikes others as foolhardy or rude.

However, by the middle school years, many girls begin to silence themselves. They are taught (and believe) the myth that loud, physical girls are not nice or attractive. So they "go underground," adapting their words and actions to what they think other people want, rather than valuing their own needs.

For parents, the trick is to promote courage in younger daughters without pushing them to be foolhardy and then help older daughters keep bravery handy as they pass into the more complicated world of adolescence.

What to Say and Do

1–7 YEARS OLD

Girls need to practice courage and experiment with their limits. When girls are young, most of this is in the physical realm.

- Let's see how far we can ride our bikes together into this really strong head-wind.

- Sure, go ahead and climb that tree. If you need any advice or cheering, I'll be right here at the bottom for you.

- It took a lot of guts for you to tell me that, even though you knew I wouldn't like to hear it. I admire your courage.

- Show me the bravest thing you know how to do.

8–13 YEARS OLD

This is the time when many girls seem to move from outspoken Bravehearts to meek mousekins. Girls don't forget how to be brave but do feel slapped down for *showing* courage. We can help them remember.

- You say you don't know how you feel, but I think you do know. I promise not to criticize how you feel, or tell anyone else. So let's talk about it.

- You are beautiful when you stand up for yourself.

- I really admire how brave you were just now. I like your courage.

- I agree; this rafting trip is scary. That's part of what will make it fun and thrilling. And I know you are brave enough to do the trip and embrace the thrills.

14 AND UP

At this age, a girl shows much of her courage by being honest in her peer relationships, especially with other girls. Encourage her to be true to herself and be honest with friends.

- I know you're struggling with what to say and what to do about this conflict with your friend. I'm here to listen anytime you want to talk it through. And I'll only give you advice if you ask for it.

- One of the toughest things I've ever learned is that I can't change someone else or how they feel. It takes courage to admit that, and courage to be honest about how you feel and what you want.

Actions to Use

- Give specific positive feedback about her courageous words and actions.

- Support and/or accompany her when she does things that require courage and risk taking.

- Be open (without bragging) about the things you do that require courage.

- Be an example of living honestly and being true to yourself, even when it's uncomfortable.

What Not to Say and Do

Don't buy into the myth that girls are the "weaker" sex and that femininity precludes boldness. Don't ridicule your daughter's fears or courage. Don't say,

- You can't do that; you're a girl.

- All girls are scared of that.

- You're just a chicken.

- Keep your mouth shut. Girls aren't allowed to say things like that.

Resources

The Blueprint for My Girls: How to Build a Life Full of Courage, Determination, & Self-Love by Yasmin Shiraz. Simon & Schuster, 2003.

Parent as Coach: Helping Your Teen Build a Life of Confidence, Courage and Compassion by Diana Haskins. Hara Publishing Group, 2002.

CREATIVITY

"Mandy came home from school the other day and wouldn't show me the drawings she had done in art class. When I asked again, she cried a little and told me that one of the other kids said she was terrible at drawing. I know she's not a great artist, but I don't want her to shut down her creative ideas."—Nita

Things to Consider

Many girls and adults don't think of themselves as creative. Creativity is often equated with being artistic or craftsy, which leaves many of us and our girls out. And while that's one definition of creativity, creativity includes much more than pure artistic talent. We're all creative in our daily lives as we make friends, solve problems, try a new way of doing something, plant a garden, cook a meal, repair a car, comfort someone, write a note, balance the family budget, or rearrange a room.

It's to your daughter's benefit to think of herself as creative in all aspects of her life. When she's facing a challenge or feeling emotionally stuck, thinking of herself as creative will greatly increase her resourcefulness in figuring out what to do. Her sense of herself as creative will be directly influenced by two things: you recognizing and celebrating her creativity in the small things she does as well as the large, and you recognizing your own creativity and sharing it with her.

What to Say and Do

1–7 YEARS OLD
In their earliest years, girls are naturally creative. Notice and celebrate her creativity in the little, everyday things.

- You thought that up all by yourself.

- You invented a new hairdo.

As she gets older and starts comparing herself to others, she'll absorb messages that make her doubt her creativity. Counter the doubts directly by pointing out the many ways she and others are creative.

- It's so neat the way you and Jeris invented that game.

- Dad came up with a whole new way to make mashed potatoes!

8–13 YEARS OLD
Focus on her unique approach to whatever she's interested in.

- You always give it your own special twist.

- The outfits you put together are so creative.

Reinforce and support her creative problem solving.

- That's a tough one, but you're so creative you'll figure it out.

- How many ideas can the four of us come up with for what to do?

14 AND UP
Encourage her to develop her creativity in many ways.

- The project you came up with for the science fair is so creative.

- Can you give me some help decorating this package?

Show her your willingness to be creative, even when it doesn't turn out the way you expected.

- Now I love the new color in the dining room even though it's much brighter than I expected.

- That tarp managed to keep the tent dry even though the way we put it up was peculiar.

- I'm glad we took the back roads to Aunt Berta's and saw that cool bridge even though we got a little lost.

Words and Phrases to Use

- Brilliant

- Inventive

- Your own way

- Brainstorm

- Why not?

- Give it a try.

- Experiment

- Unique

- Interesting

- Beautiful

- Gorgeous

What Not to Say and Do

Don't compare your daughter unfavorably to others, implying that there's something wrong or lacking in her creativity or with her ideas. Don't say,

- Look at how much more interesting Ami's project is. She's so creative.

- Just stick with the way they told you to do it.

- Your way probably won't work.

Don't limit her definition of creativity to the arts or discourage her from trying other things. Don't say,

- Anyone can cross-stitch, but painting is really creative.

- Karate isn't creative; it's just about being fit.

Resources

Creativity and Giftedness by Donald Treffinger and Sally Reis. SAGE Publications, 2004.

Magic Trees of the Mind: How to Nurture Your Child's Intelligence, Creativity, and Healthy Emotions from Birth through Adolescence by Marian Diamond and Janet Hopson. Plume, 2001.

Young at Art: Teaching Toddlers Self-Expression, Problem-Solving Skills, and an Appreciation of Art by Susan Striker. Henry Holt, 2001.

CRITICAL THINKING

"Whenever I disagree with or try to find out more about my daughter's analysis of a situation, she either gets loud and rude or else completely tunes me out. But with her friends, she seems like a church mouse, afraid to ever express an opinion."—Joselina

Things to Consider

Girls get many messages (subtle and not so subtle) that they should always be "nice." Yet at the same time, we expect girls to be intelligent and discerning. Many girls associate critical thinking with being critical, and they associate being critical with being mean.

Adults play a key role in helping girls understand the difference between critically examining a situation, belief, or behavior and tearing down another person. We do that by encouraging them to think both logically and creatively. Especially in early years, it's more important that girls practice thinking things through and asking probing questions than it is for them to have the "right" answer.

What to Say and Do

1–7 YEARS OLD

Younger girls ask a lot of "why?" questions. Encourage this behavior, even when it seems repetitive. Try to follow the path of her reasoning so you can help her learn additional ways to think.

- Why do you think Angela and Billy did that on the playground? Can you imagine whether there are other reasons why?

- What parts of this story seemed most believable to you? How come?

- What other ways can you imagine that this story could have turned out? Which one would you choose? Why?

8–13 YEARS OLD

Challenge her arguments in stimulating and constructive ways, without making it personal. Help her develop her thoughts and thought processes.

- Have you considered this point of view?

- How could you explain this opinion to someone who disagrees with you, particularly if you were trying to persuade them to change their view?

- How do you think the producers put that TV show together the way they did? What were they trying to accomplish?

14 AND UP

Many girls believe that maintaining relationships, at any cost, is their top priority. Help them understand the tyranny of always being nice and the importance of thinking for oneself.

- You can criticize someone's opinion without running them down.

- It seems like you're offended or your feelings got hurt in this discussion. Let's talk about how and why that happened.

- I like the challenging way that you examine situations, ask questions, and think things through.

- Listen to others and be considerate of their feelings. But don't let fears of hurting their feelings stop you from thinking critically and honestly about the situation.

- When you disagree with Sharon, it doesn't mean you don't like her anymore.

Words and Phrases to Use

- I'm really curious. Explain how you thought your way to that conclusion.

- I like the way you analyze things.

- What do you think of this situation?

What Not to Say and Do

Don't belittle her thought processes and beliefs. Don't say,

- How could you think such a stupid thing?

- Don't say that; it doesn't make any sense.

Don't confuse critical thinking with disparagement. Don't say,

- Are you saying I'm stupid?

- Only an idiot would think that.

Resources

Asking the Right Questions: A Guide to Critical Thinking by M. Neil Browne and Stuart M. Keeley. Prentice Hall, 2003.

Raising Thinking Children by Myrna Shure. Simon & Schuster, 1996.

DATING, CRUSHES, AND ROMANCE

"The first time a boy comes calling, I'm going to be out on the front porch just casually cleaning my shotgun. I was a boy once, and I want him to know that at least one person in this family is onto him. I know all he wants is to score."—Henry

Things to Consider

At younger ages, girls may feel superior to boys or find them simply dull. By middle school, many girls are eager to be attracted to, and to attract the attention of, boys. Meanwhile, there is enormous cultural pressure on girls to act and think in inappropriate sexual ways at younger and younger ages, long before they are developmentally ready. Girls often believe that they must hide their abilities or act passively to win boys' favor, and that pressure makes it hard for a girl to hang on to her strong self.

It's also normal for girls to get a crush or feel sexual feelings toward another girl. That doesn't necessarily mean that she is homosexual. However, it's a fact of life that some of our daughters will be lesbian, and that can be difficult for both you and her to accept. (See the "Sexual Identity" chapter for more on this topic.)

We must help girls navigate the confusing and exciting terrain of crushes and romantic feelings while staying true to themselves, their boundaries, their desires, their beliefs, and their goals. They cannot accomplish this if we (on one extreme) attempt to lock them up in a convent or (on the other extreme) let them wander without any guidance. Resorting to "cleaning my shotgun" tactics demonstrates that you don't trust her, and that undermines her ability to make smart decisions.

What to Say and Do

1–7 YEARS OLD
Encourage her to value boy peers and relatives for their traits, and not as "pretend boyfriends."

- It's fun watching you and Manuel play chess; you're getting better every time.

- You and Pete are so gentle and patient with your new baby cousin.

Dad, start early to develop strong, trusting father-daughter bonds.

- Mom needs to work now. Let's you and me go on a daddy-daughter hike!

8–13 YEARS OLD
Help her keep balance if she starts getting interested in romance. Encourage her to feel attractive and lovable for what she does and thinks, and that it's normal if she's not very interested in romance.

- You have to finish your homework and piano before you can call Stefan.

- You really kicked butt in the game tonight. I don't think Jeff could have kept up with you!

Tell her stories about when you were first interested in romance.

- It took days of talking and cheerleading from my best friend Tyler before I got up the nerve to ask a girl for my first dance.

- When I had my first crush and we danced together, I felt like I was floating!

Provide strong guidelines about dating behavior. Girls under the age of fifteen or sixteen are not ready developmentally for an intense one-on-one romantic relationship even though they may yearn for it. Let her explore romantic relationships with a lot of oversight and family involvement.

14 AND UP
Gradually give her more autonomy and accountability except where her physical or emotional safety is clearly in danger. Keep valuing her for who she is, not whether or not she has a boyfriend.

- You can go to the dance with Nils if we all agree on ground rules and consequences for breaking them. What do you think?

- This is where I need to step in as your parent.

Give her feedback on her decision making and reinforce her values and your limits.

- How honest do you feel you and Fred can be with each other?

- You handled that rough spot with Jamal really well, and you seem to be enjoying each other more now.

- You'll be able to go on one-on-one dates when you're sixteen.

Continue to focus on all of her qualities, and don't be blind to a boyfriend's good qualities. Welcome the boyfriend or girlfriend into many of your regular family activities.

- It's so sweet the way Julian talked to your little cousin.

- Can Meredith come for our family game night on Friday?

Words and Phrases to Use

- Let's have Sam over for family dinner on Sunday.

- What do you want?

- What feels right?

Actions to Use

- Tell stories about the fears, excitement, and learning of your adolescence.

- Watch that she doesn't give up all contact and time with other friends for the sake of a romance.

- Trust that your limits can help her, even if she complains about them. She can resist a lot of peer pressure by saying, "Oh, my mom would kill me if I did that. Sorry."

What Not to Say and Do

Don't give her the idea that girls and boys can't be good friends. Don't ignore her interests, abilities, and desires regarding romance.

- You shouldn't be interested in boys yet.

- You're so irresponsible.

Don't instill an overblown fear about boys in her.

- Boys can't be trusted; they only want one thing—sex.

- Boys make girls stupid.

Don't ignore or shame her feelings if she's attracted to girls. Educate yourself, get help from other parents on how to be understanding, and support her.

Don't make disparaging remarks about her boyfriend; that pushes her to have more loyalty toward him than you.

Resources

The Big Talk: Talking to Your Child about Sex and Dating by Laurie Langford. John Wiley & Sons, 1998.

Don't Bet on the Prince by Gilda Carle. St. Martin's Press, 1999.

A Smart Girl's Guide to Boys: Surviving Crushes, Staying True to Yourself and Other Stuff by Nancy Holyoke, illustrated by Bonnie Timmons. Pleasant Company Publications, 2001.

DEATH

"When my husband died, I quickly lined up a counselor for me and my two children. My ten-year-old son gets a lot from the therapy, but my thirteen-year-old daughter resists going and says, 'I don't need to talk to anyone about this.'"—Mary

Things to Consider

The death of a loved one (especially a parent or sibling) is not a one-time event for a child; its impact lasts for years. Grief can be complex for adolescent girls, who are still developing emotional awareness and may feel any emotion more intensely. But it's difficult to make sense of death and grief at any age, making our parental challenge even greater.

Be open and honest about her (and your) grief, and the ways that this death is affecting her life, even if her responses don't fit your expectations. As psychologist Dawne Kimball, PhD, says, "We expect girls to be expressive of their feelings, but not all girls are. A grieving girl may want to kick a soccer ball or drive her car until she feels in control again. What we're looking for within our families is acceptance that it's OK for each person to grieve in her own way."

Remember that grief is a natural response to death and loss, not a mental illness. However, the help of others (including professionals) can help us through grief, especially if it does trigger a mental illness like chronic depression.

What to Say and Do

1–7 YEARS OLD

You can't protect your daughter from being hurt or feeling abandoned by a loved one's death. Be realistic with her so her hurt will not remain hidden.

- Things will not be the same, and it is OK to be sad, afraid, confused, and angry about that.

- I know. I wish Papa was still here, too.

- Sheila was wrong to tease you about not having a mom. I think your teacher may have some ideas on how to help the situation; do you think we should go talk to him?

Accept that her questions may be repetitive and seem illogical. Work on following and validating her line of reasoning while giving direct, honest information.

- No, Mommy is not coming home. When someone dies, they don't come back again, like you might see on TV.

- I know you're angry at Dad for going away. You're right; it is sad and unfair that he died.

- I know you wish that you could do something to bring Daddy back. Nothing you did made him die, and nothing we do can make him not be dead. We can remember him and still love him.

- No, honey, you can't be my wife. I really love you as my daughter, and I want you to stay as my daughter. And, for now, we'll live without a momma or a wife in our family.

- It seems like this new situation is hard for you. Are you afraid because you think you might be left behind, like when Mom died?

8–13 YEARS OLD

As girls age, they can grasp some more abstract aspects of death and grieving. But they may easily slip back and forth between childish thoughts and more mature understanding.

- No one can "replace" your father. He was unique and that's why it's so heart-breaking that he's gone.

- You and I can't remove this overwhelming loss and grief about Mom. We have to feel it and talk about it to get through this. If you don't want to talk to me, I'm glad to help us find someone you feel better talking to.

- It's OK to tell Carol that Mom will always be first in your heart. Carol knows that becoming your stepmother means understanding and respecting how important Mom was and is to you. And I promise to always respect Mom, too, even after Carol and I are married.

As she grows more capable, watch that she doesn't take on parental responsibilities in order to ease the family's pain.

- You don't have to be perfect just because Mommy died. I want you to be the child and let me be the parent.

- Thank you for wanting to take care of me. Remember that Grandma and my friends are helping me a lot with my grief, so you don't have to feel responsible for me.

- I don't want you to sacrifice your friends or activities to try to help me feel better.

14 AND UP

Help her be with her grief rather than to distract herself or you away from it.

- You don't have to keep a stiff upper lip for anyone about Poppa's death.

- I feel confused and sad about this. It seems like you have strong feelings about it, too.

- Even though Mom and I got divorced, I know that her death is devastating for you. I know that our divorce was hard for you, and I am very sorry that you have to go through this loss, too. I will be here for you with whatever you need, just as your mom would have been if the tables were turned.

- It is completely OK for you and me to feel badly at the same time. We don't have to "take turns."

Acknowledge the contradictions and difficulties as she tries to make sense of the death.

- How did God let this happen? I don't know the answer. I don't know if there is an answer, and that's not very satisfying. Where do you think you can find comfort?

- It isn't easy when your friends don't understand or seem to remember what it means to you that your brother is dead.

- You don't have to act or be just like Dad to honor his memory. I want you to be yourself.

Actions to Use

- Be open about grieving and affirm her grief.

- Model expression of grief as a healthy, normal response to death and loss.

- Talk about the dead person. Remember good, bad, and in-between times you had together.

- Share stories regularly, particularly when the girl has few or no memories of her deceased family member.

- Be patient with repetitious questions.

- Reach out for help.

- Remember that there is no time period by which you should be over your grief.

- Remember to have fun together, and keep humor in your memories of the dead person.

- Use ritual to help talk about and process grief.

- Listen closely and take her seriously.

What Not to Say and Do

Don't deny the reality of her loss.

- Don't walk away from her tears or her silences.

- Don't minimize her reactions or dismiss them as illogical.

- Don't act like the dead person never existed.

Don't let your own discomfort get in the way. Don't say,

- It's all for the best; you'll see.

- You can't be sad now; Grandma will be here for dinner soon.

Words and Phrases to Avoid

- Your mom would want you to be strong.

- Your dad would want you to be over this by now.

- Don't be sad; she's in heaven!

- You need to take over the family things that Mom used to do.

- I'm too sad to listen; be a good girl and go play.

- Other people are forgetting about Daddy's death, so we should, too.

Resources

For girls:

The Fall of Freddie the Leaf by Leo F. Buscaglia. Henry Holt, 2002.

Help Me Say Goodbye: Activities for Helping Kids Cope When a Special Person Dies by Janis Silverman. Fairview Press, 1999.

Missing May by Cynthia Rylant. Yearling Books, 1993.

Walk Two Moons by Sharon Creech. HarperTrophy, 1996.

What on Earth Do You Do When Someone Dies? by Trevor Romain and Elizabeth Verdick. Free Spirit Publishing, 1999.

For adults:

A Grace Disguised: How the Soul Grows through Loss by Gerald L. Sitser. Zondervan, 1998.

Helping Children Cope with the Loss of a Loved One: A Guide for Grownups by William C. Kroen. Free Spirit Publishing, 1996.

Lifetimes: The Beautiful Way to Explain Death to Children by Bryan Mellonie. Bantam, 1983.

Motherless Daughters: The Legacy of Loss by Hope Edelman. Delta, 1995.

Mourning and Mitzvah: A Guided Journal for Walking the Mourner's Path through Grief to Healing by Anne Brener. Jewish Lights Press, 2001.

When Children Grieve: For Adults to Help Children Deal with Death, Divorce, Pet Loss, Moving, and Other Losses by John W. James and Russell Friedman. Quill, 2002.

DECISION MAKING

"Simone has trouble choosing and making decisions. She hems and haws and often just waits so long that someone else (me!) decides for her. I like it that she considers things carefully but want to help her get better at making decisions in a timely way."—Thea

Things to Consider

Even though it's much easier for us to make all the decisions, especially when she's small, we shortchange her when we don't give her a lot of opportunity to learn how to make decisions on her own, experience real-life results, and learn from them. After all, the goal of parenting is to raise our children to be responsible, fulfilled adults. And good decision making is key to both fulfillment and responsible living.

There are many skills involved in making good decisions, both emotional and intellectual, and they are learned throughout childhood. First, your girl needs to know herself—her likes, her dislikes, and her personal boundaries. She needs to have confidence in her ability to make decisions so that she won't be paralyzed by indecision. She also needs to be able to cope when a decision turns out wrong, as some decisions inevitably do. Then she has to learn how to apply logical reasoning and to weigh input from others in her decision making. Ultimately, she also has to be able to look into the future and reasonably imagine the consequences of a decision before she makes it so she can factor that into the decision. Many of these skills continue to develop in adulthood (as we parents can let her know) and throughout life, so don't expect her to be more perfect than we are.

What to Say and Do

1–7 YEARS OLD
Give her lots of opportunities to make decisions in daily life and start to develop logical thinking.

- Would you like a pear or an apple?

- Which sheets should we put on your bed?

- Do you think I should get Grandpa this card or that card?

- If we leave this plate of cheese down on the low table, what do you think the puppy will do?

8–13 YEARS OLD
Let her make more important decisions as she gets older, giving her practice.

- It's up to you to decide if you want to keep taking piano lessons.

- You can set your own bedtime during summer vacation.

Give her feedback on decision making and gradually increase the difficulty as she can handle it.

- You figured that out really well.

- It was complicated, and you thought about it a lot of different ways.

Let her experience the real consequences of the decisions she makes.

- I'm sorry your homework isn't done, but it's time to go to bed.

- You saved up, so now you can get this bike that's on sale on the spur of the moment.

14 AND UP

Give her more and more autonomy and accountability in decisions except where her physical or emotional safety is clearly in danger. Making these judgments is the trickiest part of parenting a teen.

- You'll get clothing budget money once every two months this year instead of every month.

- This is a situation where I need to step in as an adult.

Help her think through the possible results of a decision; adolescents often need help with this.

- What do you think might happen?

- Then what would you do?

- Who can tell us about the last class trip?

- If you don't take chemistry this year, when will you be able to take it?

Words and Phrases to Use

- What do you think?

- What do you want?

- What feels right?

- How will it work?

- Who have you talked with about it?

What Not to Say and Do

Don't make decisions for her when she's capable of making them on her own. Don't say,

- Just do that.

- I knew you couldn't figure it out, so I decided.

Don't overemphasize bad decisions unless they are very serious. Don't say,

- That's horrible.

- Remember what happened last time you disagreed with me?

- You're so irresponsible.

- Are you an idiot?

Resources

Parenting to Build Character in Your Teen by Michael Josephson, Tom Dowd, and Val Peter. Boys Town Press, 2001.

Smart Choices: A Practical Guide to Making Better Decisions by John Hammond, Ralph Keeney, and Howard Raiffa. Broadway Books, 2002.

DEPRESSION

"Lately Miranda seems to have less energy and fun than she used to. She says she's bored a lot and is spending more time watching TV. The phone doesn't seem to be ringing as much with her friends calling, and when I ask if she wants to invite someone over, she says, 'Maybe,' but then doesn't do it. She's doing fine in school gradewise, and I don't want to make a big deal out of normal preteen behavior. But I'm worried that she might be depressed, and I don't know how to tell if she needs help."—Fritzie

Things to Consider

Unfortunately, depression is fairly common in preteen and teen girls (more than in boys). Girls often turn their anger inside (instead of expressing it directly). Major life changes or traumas like parental divorce or a family or friend death often cause depression (which is expected in such situations). The constantly changing social constellation of these years is confusing and can worsen feelings of loneliness, which are somewhat normal developmentally.

Parents need to be attuned to subtle signs of depression, like withdrawal from friends and family, less interest in activities she used to enjoy, changes in appetite, increased crying, self-mutilation, experimentation with alcohol, drugs, sex, or smoking, feelings of hopelessness, increased boredom, and negative thoughts. Preteens and teens usually don't realize they are depressed and need you to identify the signs.

If you suspect that your daughter is even slightly depressed, get professional help, starting with her doctor. Talk to the doctor before you bring her in so the doctor is ready to ask specific questions that can uncover depression. Consider family therapy. At the very least, you and she will both know that you are paying close attention to her emotional well-being. And at the most, getting her help early in depression greatly increases the chance of a successful outcome for counseling.

What to Say and Do

8–13 YEARS OLD
Accept all of her feelings and provide many chances for her to talk openly about them, both ups and downs.

- You seem a little sad today. What's happening?

- Tell me about it.

Encourage her to explore and express her feelings, even if you may feel uncomfortable with them. Show her how you accept and express your sad and angry feelings.

- How can you tell your friend that you're angry about that?

- I feel a lot better after telling you how I feel.

14 AND UP
Empathize with how she's feeling and reassure her that it's not unusual. Share your experience with depression if you think that might be helpful.

- I understand you don't like feeling this way.

- We can do some things to help. That's what I do when I'm down.

- Does it feel hard to do anything today?

Give her clear messages that getting help for depression is healthy and normal to do.

- Dr. Cathy will know what we can do much better than I do.

- Times like this are when families and friends help each other out.

Words and Phrases to Use

- I hear you.
- I understand.
- I feel that way sometimes.
- When I feel sad . . .
- When I feel helpless . . .
- Normal

- Everyone feels down sometimes.
- Talking
- I'm listening.
- Get help.
- I'm glad you told me . . .

What Not to Say and Do

Don't shut down or ignore her sad or helpless feelings. Don't say,

- It's not so bad. Just smile and you'll feel better.
- I don't want to hear you talk like that.

Don't make depression seem like something to be ashamed of. Don't say,

- Don't tell anyone outside the family.
- No one should know about this.
- I don't know why you feel like that; you're so fortunate.

Words and Phrases to Avoid

- It's nothing.
- Just think positive.
- What's the matter with you?
- You're such a pessimist.

- Lighten up.

- Don't take everything so seriously.

Resources

Help Me, I'm Sad: Childhood and Teen Depression by David Fassler and Lynne Dumas. Penguin, 1998.

Overcoming Teen Depression: A Guide for Parents by Miriam Kaufman. Firefly Books, 2001.

The Secret Strength of Depression by Frederic F. Flach. Hatherleigh Press, 2003.

When Someone You Love Is Depressed by Laura Epstein Rosen. Simon & Schuster, 1997.

Teens and Therapy: www.teens-and-therapy.com

DIETING AND EATING DISORDERS

"My nine-year-old daughter looks fine to me, so I was stumped and scared when she said, 'Daddy, do you think I look fat?' What should I tell her?"
—Michael

Things to Consider

First, recognize that both answers to her question are wrong. What's wrong is the question.

Ask your daughter *why* she is asking that question, and then challenge the assumptions behind it. Chances are she's worried that she doesn't fit into the narrow and distorted "beauty" standards she sees all around her. Listen to her answers, draw her out, and take her seriously.

Girls see fat (and even slightly plump) people made fun of and discriminated against. They absorb the message that body fat is a sign of weakness and inferiority. They hear people rating body parts on a scale of 1–10. They hear other girls and women constantly criticizing their bodies and saying they need to lose weight. They grow up in a culture that treats women's (and increasingly men's) bodies as self-improvement projects that are never good enough. They learn that our culture ignores the fact that the shape of our bodies is more determined by genetics than by willpower.

They see their body size as something they should be able to control, if they really work at it. When things feel out of control in their lives, they may try to cope by turning to dieting or eating disorders like starvation (anorexia), purging (bulimia), compulsive exercising, or compulsive overeating.

What to Say and Do

1–7 YEARS OLD
Girls need to learn early and often that their bodies are valuable for what they do (think, run, build, pretend, feel, and so on) rather than their shape, size, or color.

- It's exciting to see how much better you're riding your bike.

- I think what you said is very interesting. Tell me more.

- Let's build and play today. What clothes would be best for us to wear?

8–13 YEARS OLD
Girls often worry that they don't fit into the narrow "beauty" standards (99 percent external) they see among peers, in stores, and in media.

- Why are you asking me if I think you look fat? Where is that question coming from?

- The photos you see in *Seventeen* and *YM* are computer altered, and those magazines work to make you feel crummy so you'll buy the stuff they advertise.

- If someone told you that you had to be two feet taller by next month, you'd laugh at them. Your shape and mine are just as genetic as our height.

14 AND UP
The pressure to swallow the beauty myth can intensify as a girl emerges sexually.

- Physical attraction is great; I was physically attracted to your mother when I first met her. But that alone can't sustain a romantic relationship and never will.

- There's a word for judging people by how they look: *bigotry.* There is no excuse for it.

- You are beautiful when you stand up for yourself.

Actions to Use

- Give specific positive feedback about her accomplishments and thoughts.

- Use stories and photos to show her how earlier generations of your family looked and what they accomplished. This demonstrates concretely how genetics ultimately determine our height, skin color, shape, and other physical attributes.

- Be physically active with her: shoot hoops, play catch, ride bikes together, play chess, or go for a walk.

- Put your daughter's face in the picture when looking at marketing aimed at girls. If you don't like what you see, raise hell with the marketer.

What Not to Say and Do

Don't diet yourself or encourage her to diet unless your doctor gives a reasonable medical reason to do so. Don't say,

- That will make you fat.

- Do you really want that much?

- Aren't you full?

- Don't eat like a pig.

Words, Phrases, and Actions to Avoid

- God, I look fat.

- She looks disgusting.

- Seeing body shape as a sign of willpower or moral fiber

Resources

Body Wars: Making Peace with Women's Bodies by Margo Maine. Gurze Books, 2000.

Real Kids Come in All Sizes: Ten Essential Lessons to Build Your Child's Body Esteem by Kathy Kater. Broadway Books, 2004.

The Solution by Laurel Mellin. Regan Books, 1997.

When Girls Feel Fat: Helping Girls through Adolescence by Sandra Susan Friedman. Firefly Books, 2000.

A Very Hungry Girl: How I Filled Up on Life . . . and How You Can, Too! by Jessica Weiner. Hay House, 2003.

National Eating Disorders Association: www.nationaleatingdisorders.org

Eating Disorders Coalition: www.eatingdisorderscoalition.org

DISAGREEMENTS

*"Sachi doesn't like any kind of conflict. She takes it all personally and gets eas-
ily hurt whenever a friend or family member doesn't agree with her. Is there
any way to help her handle it better?"—Jun*

Things to Consider

Young girls usually don't have any trouble expressing their disagreements with you,
their siblings, or their friends. But as girls get a bit older, they receive subtle clues that
it's not nice to disagree because they might hurt someone's feelings. They start to limit
direct talking about conflict and lose awareness of their own points of view. How many
times have you heard your older daughter say, "I don't know," in response to a question
about her opinion or feelings?

At the same time that girls become less able to directly disagree with others, they
become more sensitive to others disagreeing with them and take it more personally.
Turning a disagreement into a judgment is unhelpful in relationships, and it contributes
to the emotionally hurtful and indirect ways that preadolescent and adolescent girls
handle conflict by exclusion, gossip, and betrayal.

Giving your daughter strong, consistent support for respectfully voicing her
opinions and feelings is the best thing you can do to counteract these pressures. You
also need to help her learn to separate her sense of self from the disagreements others
have with her and realize that she can learn from disagreements. Girls who can express

their own opinions and feelings and also listen to those who disagree with their opinions will be better able to get along with others while remaining true to themselves.

What to Say and Do

1–7 YEARS OLD
Point out how she is able to both voice and listen to disagreement.

- I like the way you and Tyrone listened to each other when you wanted to play different games and then took turns.

Ask her opinion about big and small things and allow her to disagree with you even though you still make the final decision.

- How do you feel about missing practice so we can go to Frannie's recital?

8–13 YEARS OLD
Provide strong support for her continuing to voice disagreement when she feels it.

- I'm glad you told me how you feel. It's important to do that, even when I don't agree.

- I know it's hard to tell Grace that you disagree, but it's important to be honest.

Help her practice disagreeing with others in a productive, respectful way. Model respectful disagreement with your friends and family.

- Let's try different ways you can tell Leah that you don't want to go to the movie.

- When you told Annie how you felt without blaming her, she listened and understood you better.

Show her how you can accept disagreement, not take it personally, and learn from the other person's perspective. Help her practice this skill, too.

- Mom and I don't agree with each about what's fair, so we're working out a compromise. She brought up some things I hadn't thought about.

- You really don't like this? Tell me why.

14 AND UP

Welcome her respectful disagreement with you. Ask her to back up her opinions with facts and persuasion.

- We disagree about eating meat. Tell me why you think it's not healthy and where we can learn more.

When disagreement is based on feelings rather than facts, listen carefully to understand her perspective and teach her to do that for others.

- I hear that you feel very anxious about the test even though you've studied hard. I think you'll do fine.

- I agree that it doesn't make any sense that Jessica would feel angry at you about that, but she does. I wonder why?

Words and Phrases to Use

- What do you think?
- How do you feel?
- Tell me about it.
- That's your opinion.
- I respect your opinion.

- Explain it to me.
- Agree to disagree.
- Perspective
- Walk a mile in her shoes.
- A different view

What Not to Say and Do

Don't stifle her disagreement with you even though you will still make the final decision. Don't say,

■ Don't tell me whether you like it or not; it's just the way it is.

■ Where did you get such a silly idea?

Don't tell her (directly or indirectly) to avoid disagreement and conflict. Don't say,

■ Don't tell Gram that; it will hurt her feelings.

■ Bill will feel like an idiot if you disagree with him about that.

■ If you can't say anything nice, don't say anything at all.

Resources

How Can You Say That? What to Say to Your Daughter When One of You Just Said Something Awful by Amy Lynch. Pleasant Company Publications, 2003.

How to Negotiate with Kids Even When You Think You Shouldn't by Scott Brown. Penguin, 2004.

DIVORCE

"My husband and I are getting divorced, and we're having some serious problems agreeing on how to deal with our daughter Paige. As a matter of fact,
we're having trouble agreeing on almost anything these days. Meanwhile,
Paige is sometimes moping, sometimes acting out, and sometimes trying to
be the peacemaker, and her school performance is dropping."—Taralyn

Things to Consider

When it comes to divorce's impact on a girl, her parents carry the primary responsibility. You must acknowledge that divorce brings a lot of change and emotion to *everyone*
in your immediate and extended family. Communicate directly with each other and
your children. Explicitly say that the divorce is not the kids' fault, and that both parents
will continue to love and care for them, no matter what. Then, live up to that commitment every day.

Don't try to buy her love with things, even if your ex does. Your daughter needs
your presence, not your presents. Never bad-mouth your ex in front of your children. A
girl needs to witness ongoing respect for female and male character. She particularly
needs the continued positive involvement of *both* parents and any stepparents who
enter her life.

Your daughter and your ex are different people. Don't misdirect anger at your ex
toward your daughter. When your daughter does not listen, does less than her best in

school, or makes other blunders (normal behaviors for most kids), be careful not to confuse her mistakes with your ex's actions, and instead, see what *you* can do to make things better.

Finally, recognize that successful divorced parents are among the most attentive parents there are. They are innovators in being attuned to their kids, consciously sacrificing and scheduling time to be with them, and being creative and consistent in their parent-child communication. These are qualities every parent should aspire to!

What to Say and Do

1–7 YEARS OLD

Younger girls may be especially susceptible to the idea that they caused the divorce. Give your daughter consistent time and healthy attention in person, on the phone, over the Internet, through the mail, or any other way.

- I think what you said is very interesting. Tell me more.

- How are you feeling? What do you wish would happen?

- I want you to love and be close to your mother/father. That doesn't hurt me; it makes me happy.

- What do you want to do with our time together?

- Our divorce is not your fault. Nothing you did made it happen.

Communicate with her *every* day.

8–13 YEARS OLD

Listen and be there for her. Accept your daughter for who she is, not who you want her to be, think she should be, or think she would be if she were raised only by you. She may naturally grieve and be moody just before and after she leaves your house and your ex's house. Keep being affectionate even if she's moody.

- I can't guarantee that everything will be OK. But I can guarantee that I will always be loyal to you.

- It's OK to be upset when you leave your other house and family. How can I help?

- There are bound to be different rules in your two homes. The only rules you and I can control are the ones here, so let's not waste energy on the other house's rules.

- You're not responsible for problems between your father/mother and me, so don't try to fix them. We grown-ups are responsible for that.

14 AND UP

As girls get more autonomous, they may think they have the power to fix your broken relationship (the *Parent Trap* myth). As they emerge sexually, it is vital that they have healthy relationships with all of their parents and stepparents.

- Even though our marriage didn't work out, there were many good things about the beginning of our relationship. Let me tell you some stories from back then.

- I love you for who you are. You are special and loveable. That doesn't change because your parents got divorced.

- I'm here for the long haul.

- Our divorce was our decision and is our responsibility. Your responsibility is to be part of healthy relationships with each of us.

Actions to Use

- When spending time and/or talking together, focus on her and her life rather than on your problems or troubles with your ex.

- Talk well about your daughter's other parent(s) even when you're angry at them, and even if they speak poorly about you.

- Resolve adult conflicts away from your daughter and allow her to be the child.

- Remember that it takes two people to fight. If power struggles and arguments with your ex get in the way of your relationship with your daughter, then stop participating in them.

- Focus on your daughter's positives. Focusing on negatives undermines your daughter's strength and confidence—strength and confidence already stretched by living in two homes.

- Develop healthy social and emotional supports for yourself. Be careful not to become emotionally dependent on your daughter. Instead, spend time with healthy adults and get your emotional and social needs met through them.

- Keep grandparents, cousins, aunts, uncles, family friends, and other extended "family" involved in her life as much as possible.

What Not to Say and Do

Don't *ever* break a promise about when you'll visit, call, or do anything else she's counting on you to do. Don't dismiss her feelings about the divorce or blame her for it in any way. Don't say,

- Your mother/father and I wouldn't have these problems if you just behaved yourself!

- Don't be upset by the divorce.

- I'm not going to let you come back here if you don't shape up.

- Your mother/father is an idiot; I don't know why I ever married her/him.

- Don't worry; everything will be OK and you don't have to feel bad.

- I have to be your father and your mother. (You can only be yourself and bring her all the strengths you have; don't also try to be her "mother" or her "father," whatever you may think that means.)

Actions to Avoid

- Don't use your daughter to get back at your ex.

- Avoid negative talk about her other parent.

- Never use your daughter to work out your emotional problems or to get your adult relationship needs met.

- Don't demand or force your daughter to immediately accept and love a new stepparent.

(Some of this section is adapted from "Ten Tips for Live-Away Dads" written by William C. Klatte for the nonprofit Dads and Daughters [www.dadsanddaughters.org], copyrighted by Dads and Daughters and used by permission. They work just as well for divorced moms.)

Resources

Help! A Girl's Guide to Divorce and Stepfamilies by Nancy Holyoke, illustrated by Scott Nash. Pleasant Company Publications, 1999.

How to Survive Your Parents' Divorce: Kids' Advice to Kids by Gayle Kimball. Equality Press, 1994.

Live-Away Dads: Staying a Part of Your Children's Lives When They Aren't a Part of Your Home by William C. Klatte. Penguin, 1999.

Making Divorce Easier on Your Child: 50 Effective Ways to Help Children Adjust by Nicholas Long and Rex L. Forehand. McGraw-Hill, 2002.

What about the Kids? Raising Your Children Before, During, and After Divorce by Judith S. Wallerstein and Sandra Blakeslee. Hyperion, 2003.

DRINKING, DRUGS, AND SMOKING

"I thought I smelled cigarette smoke on Angie's clothes when she came in last night. This morning, I looked for them, but she'd already put them in the laundry. We've always stressed how bad smoking is and how we wish that Uncle Will and Aunt Sarah didn't smoke. She's a very smart girl. Why would she do this?"—Darla

Things to Consider

Smoking, alcohol abuse, and drug use are among the scariest issues we parents confront with our daughters. We don't want them to be harmed or endangered by doing these things, and we don't even want them to experiment with them. But we need to face the reality that most girls will experiment with one or all of these dangerous things, through the influence of peers, curiosity, rebelliousness, or an emotional need.

Age twelve to fourteen is the typical age for first experimentation, often as a way to fit in or seem cool during the stressful social times of middle school. A girl's experimentation can be a chance for her to decide she doesn't like the way it feels and that she doesn't want to do it. If you've given her the practice and understanding to make decisions in her own best interest, the experiment is likely to end without a habit developing.

All three habits are similar in their root causes, unhealthy effects, and potential for addiction. Clearly, we can't monitor our daughters all the time to prevent these habits. We need to start early building the foundation for them to have healthy ways to cope with stress and her emotions. We also need to provide them with the health facts on each subject, separate from any moral views we may have about them. (Research has shown that many girls start to smoke because they mistakenly believe it will keep their weight down.) The most powerful thing we can do to safeguard our daughters against these habits is to not do them ourselves. So if you smoke, use drugs, or abuse alcohol, change your own behavior, talk about it, and show your daughter what you are doing while you teach her how to avoid the pitfalls that you fell into.

What to Say and Do

1–7 YEARS OLD

Put the emphasis on taking care of your own health and let her see how you do that by not using tobacco or drugs or abusing alcohol.

- I get a headache when I'm in smoky rooms, so I avoid them.

- I get dizzy when I drink more than one glass of wine at a time, so I don't do that.

8–13 YEARS OLD

Start providing factual (not sensational) information about the health risks of use and abuse.

- Smoking is addictive and causes heart attacks, cancer, and lots of other problems.

- Drugs aren't all addictive, but you can get so you rely on them emotionally, which is just as unhealthy.

Be honest about your family's past or present use of alcohol, tobacco, or drugs. If you're currently using or abusing any of them, it's more likely that she will too, and it will be much harder to make the case for why she shouldn't.

- Auntie is a recovering alcoholic and can't stop once she starts drinking, so she doesn't drink any alcohol at all. She had a terrible accident once when she was drunk, and that motivated her to go to AA and get sober.

- I tried pot when I was in college. It felt sort of interesting to get high, but smoking the joint made my lungs burn and the high wasn't worth it. Another time a friend baked some into brownies. We ate the whole pan and it made us throw up.

14 AND UP

Pay close attention to signs that she's abusing any substance. Seek professional help right away if you think that's happening.

- I smell smoke on your clothes. Have you been smoking?

- I've made an appointment with the doctor to talk about what to do.

Support her when she talks about the social pressure to use and how it's hard to resist.

- I'm proud of you for doing what you think is right.

- It sounds like you're worried about the way Ryan drinks. It would be good for us to talk with him and his parents about it.

Words and Phrases to Use

- It's hard not to go along with the others.

- You can always call me and I'll come get you, no questions asked.

- You can tell your friends it's my fault that you can't do it. I don't mind taking the blame to keep you healthy.

- What would you say if everyone else at the party was drinking and they wanted you to?

- Responsible

- Trust

What Not to Say and Do

Don't blame her for experimenting or for telling you about it and asking you questions. Don't say,

- I don't ever want to hear about you drinking again.

- That's it! You can never hang out with Maura again.

Don't shame her if she develops a problem and needs help to stop. Don't say,

- You're a loser. I always knew it.

- Why did you do this to us?

- You've given the whole family a bad reputation.

Words and Phrases To Avoid

- No self-discipline
- Don't tell me that.

- Ashamed
- Follower

- Weak
- Spineless

Resources

Dear Kids of Alcoholics by Lindsey Hall, Leigh Cohn, and Rosemary E. Lingenfelter. Gurze Books, 1998.

Don't Let Your Kids Kill You: A Guide for Parents of Drug and Alcohol Addicted Children by Charles Rubin. New Century, 2003.

Taking Charge of My Mind and Body: A Girls' Guide to Outsmarting Alcohol, Drug, Smoking, and Eating Problems by Gladys Folkers, Elizabeth Verdick (Editor), and Jeanne Engelmann. Free Spirit Publishing, 1997.

Teens under the Influence: The Truth about Kids, Alcohol, and Other Drugs—How to Recognize the Problem and What to Do about It by Katherine Ketcham and Nicholas A. Pace. Random House, 2003.

Students Against Destructive Decisions: www.sadd.org

DRIVING

"Briana can't wait to get her driver's license as soon as possible (she's fifteen now). I must admit the thought of her driving a car by herself terrifies me, and not just because I'm the protective dad. She's a good kid, but she doesn't always show the most mature judgment. Is it unreasonable to tell her she has to wait until she's older to get her license?"—Antwone

Things to Consider

Getting your license is one of the great American rites of passage. And many parents look forward to reducing the hours they spend driving the car pool. But the fact is that teen drivers cause more accidents than drivers of any other age, due to their inexperience and sense of physical infallibility. Because inexperience or poor judgment when driving can be a life-or-death matter, it's perfectly reasonable for you to restrict driving until you feel your daughter is ready to do it responsibly.

The determination of when she's ready should not be based purely on her age. It must also include how long she's been driving regularly with adult supervision (a minimum of one year is common), what driving conditions she's experienced in (rain, snow, wind, and ice), how much she knows about car maintenance and handling on-the-road emergencies, and how well she exercises good judgment about safety issues. Many states have come to a similar conclusion in recent years and have enacted more restrictions on how early teens can get their license, increasing the age for driving at night and limiting the number of teens who can ride in a car driven by a teen. Even if your state hasn't changed the rules yet, you can set the rules for your own daughter's driving.

What to Say and Do

14 AND UP

Make it clear that you will decide when she can get her license and what your decision will be based on.

- After you pass driver's ed and have driven with us for a full year, we'll see if we think you're ready to get your license.

- Maturity is an important part of getting your license, and we'll decide that based on how you handle decisions in general.

Be matter-of-fact and open about the costs and risks of driving and how she can reduce them.

- A lot of crashes happen when drivers are distracted by something like tuning the radio or talking or when they're drowsy.

- When you get your license, our car insurance will go up by 40 percent, even if you never have an accident. That's because teen drivers in general have so many accidents. We don't want you to be one of them.

- Driving on rain, snow, and ice are incredibly tricky. Even after doing it for twenty-five years, I have to get back in practice every winter and remind myself of the techniques.

- Never drive under the influence or ride with a driver who has been drinking alcohol, even one beer.

When she gets her license, set clear limits and enforce them dispassionately. If she breaks a driving rule, take away the privilege for a proportional length of time. And of course, drive safely yourself.

Words and Phrases to Use

- Privilege
- Safety
- Anticipation
- Experience
- Judgment

- Freedom is earned through responsibility.
- Risks
- Trust
- Maturity

What Not to Say and Do

Don't give her mixed messages about the importance of driving safely.

Don't back off the rules you make for her driving and use of the car.

Don't excuse your own unsafe driving by saying you can do it because you're a better driver.

- I can speed because I know how to handle the car.

Actions to Avoid

- Don't curse at other drivers.
- Never drive unsafely yourself.
- Avoid constant criticism of her driving while she's learning.

Resources

Auto Repair for Dummies by Deanna Sclar. John Wiley & Sons, 1999.

The Isaac Newton School of Driving: Physics and Your Car by Barry Parker. Johns Hopkins University Press, 2003.

Mothers Against Drunk Driving: www.madd.org

EMBARRASSMENT

"Caroline hates to feel embarrassed. She seems to shrink right before my eyes. This happens even for small things like wearing the 'wrong' barrettes in her hair. I know just how she feels because I was the same way. I don't want her to take as long to get over small embarrassments as I did."—Gretchen

Things to Consider

Embarrassment has its positive side by keeping us from doing something that would harm us (or others). But avoidance of embarrassment can stifle a girl's development of her unique personality and weaken a healthy adventuresome nature. For girls, trying to avoid embarrassment can be a huge motivation, especially at the developmental stages when they have a somewhat fragile sense of self. Knowing how to accept and cope with embarrassment, and even learn from it, is a valuable skill for us to help girls develop. To go after what she really wants in life, she'll need to be able to endure some embarrassment.

Some girls are more sensitive and more easily embarrassed than others. If your daughter seems to want to avoid even the smallest embarrassment from a young age, it's likely that at least one of her parents is the same way. Help her develop healthy ways to fight her fear of embarrassment so it doesn't limit her. Show or tell her that what she thinks about herself is more important than what others think of her.

What to Say and Do

1–7 YEARS OLD
Gently make light of embarrassing situations that happen to you, showing her that they're part of everyone's life.

- I was embarrassed, but it was so funny when I realized my zipper was down.

- My face was so red I felt like an apple!

When she feels embarrassed, help her recover her balance with empathy and support.

- That was embarrassing but it's over now.

- You felt embarrassed when you fell. I'm proud you got up and back in the game.

- You were so excited you couldn't stay quiet. That's OK.

8–13 YEARS OLD
Fear of embarrassing moments is a big thing with this age. When she's ready, it's healthy to laugh with her about an embarrassing situation.

- That was so silly; it makes me smile just thinking about it.

If she's easily embarrassed, you need to be especially sensitive, help her understand her feelings, and work through the embarrassment in an affirming way.

- That was embarrassing. You hung in there and you handled it really well.

- I know it felt like everyone was laughing at you, but they were really laughing more at themselves and thinking about their own embarrassing moments.

- It sounds like Tara embarrasses other girls because she feels insecure. How can you remind yourself it's not about you?

14 AND UP
Support her courage to do things she wants to even though she might feel embarrassed.

- Hanging out with Danae even though she dresses differently from the other kids is brave.

- If you make a mistake in your speech, it will feel embarrassing for a minute, but no will care about it later if you recover and keep going.

- You don't know what will happen, but you do know you can handle it.

Words and Phrases to Use

- I understand.

- What has you nervous?

- What might happen?

- What would you do?

- Life is embarrassing.

- You can handle it.

- Silly things happen.

- One way to completely avoid embarrassment is to do nothing, but that's boring!

What Not to Say and Do

Don't underestimate the power of embarrassment. Don't say,

- It's no big deal.

- Why do you care about being embarrassed?

Don't emphasize her embarrassment or laugh at it if she's feeling hurt by it. Don't say,

- Just laugh at yourself.

- You looked ridiculous.

- I couldn't stop laughing.

- What a loser.

Words and Phrases to Avoid

- Get over it.

- You're too sensitive.

- You overreact.

Resources

Dying of Embarrassment by Barbara G. Markway, Alec Pollard, Cheryl N. Carmin, and Teresa Flynn. New Harbinger, 1992.

I Can't Believe I Just Did That! How (Seemingly) Small Moments of Shame and Embarrassment Can Wreak Havoc in Your Life—and What You Can Do to Put a Stop to Them by David Allyn. Tarcher, 2003.

My Worst Days Diary by Suzanne Altman, illustrated by Diane Allison. Gareth Stevens, 1996.

FAILURE

"Serena gets easily discouraged when something doesn't go the way she expected. It's like she gets blown off course and it takes her a while to adjust. She takes disappointment to heart, and often she just refuses to try again, not wanting to fail. What can I do to help her see that failure and disappointment are just part of life and don't have to be devastating?"—Winona

Things to Consider

Try, try again is a cliché because it's the story of most of our lives. Often your daughter won't get what she wants the first or even the second time around. She can learn a great deal about how to succeed on the third or fourth try if she observes her failures and looks for what caused them.

Disappointment, on the other hand, is usually due to circumstances beyond her control. Disappointment can teach her how to accept the fact that she is powerless in some circumstances. When handling it well, she can detach from the things she is powerless over and focus her energy on what she can affect.

What to Say and Do

1–7 YEARS OLD

Support her natural willingness to keep trying until she succeeds.

- You did it. Good for you!

- Let's give it another try.

Comment when she keeps trying even after failing, no matter what the ultimate result.

- I knew you could do it.

- The third time was the charm.

- It didn't work, but I'm proud of you for trying so hard.

8–13 YEARS OLD

Coach her on how she can learn from failure and improve her chance of success next time.

- Do you think it might work better another way?

- That was so close. Adjust a little and you'll have it!

Acknowledge and help her accept and process feelings of disappointment.

- It's hard to lose the game when your team tried so hard.

- I know you wish you could go on that trip. It's disappointing.

Help her accept her powerlessness when she needs to.

- On a team, you can do what you can, but the rest is up to the whole team.

- Who wins the drawing is determined by luck. There's nothing you can do about it.

14 AND UP

Give her strong encouragement and appropriate support to keep going in the face of failures. It's harder for her to do in her teens.

- Getting a C in English really upset you. I know you can turn that around with your determination and hard work. How can I help?

- You wanted the lead in the play, but Monica got it. You can make the most of the part you have and do a really great job with it.

Accepting disappointments is also more difficult now, so keep giving her support and being open about how you do it yourself.

- I'm so disappointed that I didn't get the promotion. I want to talk about it and get over it so I can decide what to do now.

- Feeling disappointed sometimes is natural. Even so, it can't take away your dreams for yourself.

Words and Phrases to Use

- You did it.
- Persistence
- Follow-through
- Give it a go.
- Try hard.
- Your best

- Let go.
- Accept
- Learn
- Adjust
- Why not?

What Not to Say and Do

Don't encourage her to give up just because she's failed at something once or twice. Don't say,

- You'll never do it since it didn't work this time.

- I think it's too hard for you.

Don't shield her from (or make false excuses for) the normal failures and disappointments of life. Experiencing and bouncing back from them is how she develops inner strength and confidence. Don't say,

- You'll just be disappointed, so why bother?

- You only lost because of that stupid ref.

Words and Phrases to Avoid

- Never

- That's too hard.

- Your chances are practically none.

- Do you really think you can do it?

- Our family never had good luck.

- Never a fair shake

Resources

The Resilience Factor: 7 Keys to Finding Your Inner Strength and Overcoming Life's Hurdles by Karen Reivich and Andrew Shatte. Broadway Books, 2003.

The Survivor Personality: Why Some People Are Stronger, Smarter, and More Skillful at Handling Life's Difficulties . . . And How You Can Be, Too by Al Siebert. Perigee, 1996.

FAITH AND SPIRITUALITY

"Dyann asks me about the 'big questions' of life, like where do we come from and why do certain things happen. She has an interest in spiritual things that I'd like to encourage. My wife and I have a strong belief in moral behavior and doing good. We're not big on organized religion and it seems kind of hard to pass on faith and spirituality on our own."—Clement

Things to Consider

Nurturing your daughter's sense of faith and spirituality can be done in many ways. Joining a religious congregation or group is the most common way parents do this, but families can take a less traditional approach. Either way, our goal is to give our daughters the strong foundation of spiritual practices that can help them find answers to life's big questions and find their part in the big picture.

Share your spiritual path with your daughter and talk about its ups and downs. Let her know how you come to spiritual decisions and find guidance from your spiritual practice. Spiritual practice can include attending religious services, reading and studying religious texts, praying, meditating, serving others, journaling, solitude, and retreats to deepen self-knowledge, or family rituals like saying grace before meals. Observe what types of spiritual practices engage her, and provide more of those opportunities. Ask her about her beliefs and doubts. Keep an open conversation going about spirituality and faith as part of daily life.

What to Say and Do

1–7 YEARS OLD
Teach her your spiritual practices by sharing them with her. Keep explanations simple.

- Let's say three things we're each thankful for before I tuck you into bed.

- I'm praying to God for help to figure out what to do.

- I believe that there's a strong energy for good in the world.

Encourage her questions about religion and spirituality.

- I'm glad you asked. Here's what I believe. Other religions might believe differently.

8–13 YEARS OLD
Try to describe your experiences of faith and spirituality in her language.

- When I'm feeling close to God, I have a peaceful feeling in my heart.

- After meditating I feel ready for whatever might happen.

- If I'm confused about something, taking a walk in the park helps me sort it out.

- Sometimes it takes a lot of asking myself questions and waiting until I feel I have an answer. It can be hard to wait until the answer arrives.

- Dad and I feel that donating to causes we believe in is important. That way we're sharing what we have.

Teach her to respect other religions and spiritual practices. Tell her about the many similarities between various spiritual traditions and beliefs.

Be aware of how your spiritual practices treat women and the messages that attitude sends your daughter.

- Our religion hasn't had women as leaders yet, but there are people working on that and I support that. I want to work for the change as part of the community.

Ask her about her beliefs, faith, and spirituality in an open way.

- Do you have a belief about that?

- What's your spiritual feeling about that?

14 AND UP

She may reject some or all of your spiritual practices as she seeks to define her own path. Understand that she needs to find her own way to spirituality and faith at this age.

- You can decide how much you will be involved in church now.

- I trust that you can figure this out for yourself now.

- I'm always here to listen when you want to talk about it.

Words and Phrases to Use

- Spirit
- Goodness
- Finding your spiritual path
- Growing spiritually

- Faith
- Belief
- Values

What Not to Say and Do

Don't force her to adopt your spiritual practices and beliefs. Don't say,

- It's not up to you.

- It's for your own good. I know best.

- You'll go to hell if you don't do this.

Don't speak badly of other religions or spiritual practices. Don't say,

- Those people are all sinners.

- They're wrong because they don't believe what we do.

Words and Phrases to Avoid

- There's only one right way to be religious.

- It's not scientific so it's nonsense.

- Punishment

- Religion is stupid.

- There's no such thing as God.

- No one can prove that spirituality makes things better.

- Faith is just an illusion.

Resources

Girlosophy: A Soul Survival Kit by Anthea Paul. Allen & Unwin, 2001.

Real Kids, Real Faith: Practices for Nurturing Children's Spiritual Lives by Karen Marie Yust. Jossey-Bass, 2004.

Soul Searching: A Girl's Guide to Finding Herself by Sarah Stillman and Susan Gross. Beyond Words Publishing, 2000.

FEAR OF GROWING UP

"When I was a girl, I couldn't wait to be older and have more freedom. So it really surprised me when my younger daughter (nine years old) told me the other day that she doesn't want to grow up. She's worried about how she'll take care of herself and about all the unknowns. She also says that she likes things the way they are now and doesn't want them to change. Should I be concerned about this?"—Ellen

Things to Consider

It may be that your daughter is more sensitive to her feelings than many children. If so, she may be concerned that she'll lose things she likes (security, no homework or chores, lack of adult responsibility) as she grows up, even as she gains the freedom and autonomy she wants. Introspective girls can have more insight and awareness than we expect at a given age. And sometimes that "more adult" awareness can be a bit of a burden for a girl. It can also be a reflection of seeing older siblings or parents lament the loss of their childhood. In any case, listen respectfully to her fears, let her know if you share them, and then help her explore them logically by looking at the pros and cons of growing up.

At the same time, if you feel that your daughter is fearful to the point of obsession and that her fear is interfering with her daily life or causing depression, she may benefit from professional help. You can get help in a matter-of-fact way without making a big deal about it. Call her doctor for a referral to a therapist, and visit with the therapist yourself before bringing her in for a joint appointment. Explain to your daughter that you and she are going to go to talk with someone who can help figure out the fear. And if you have strong fears about her growing up (most parents do), talk to a therapist yourself to be sure you're not projecting your fears onto her.

What to Say and Do

8–13 YEARS OLD
Acknowledge and accept her feeling of fear.

- It sounds like you feel worried.

- What do you think might happen?

Help her express her mixed feelings of anticipation and dread.

- You'd like to have grown-up privileges but still be taken care of.

- It can be hard to know how you'll feel before it happens.

Reassure her that you're confident she'll be ready for it by the time she's grown up and that your support will continue as long as she needs it.

- Growing up is a gradual thing. Remember when you didn't like riding your bike in the street but now you feel fine doing that?

- You can take all the time you need to get grown up. We'll be here to help.

- Family and friends will always be there for you, even when you're grown up.

14 AND UP
Her fears and sense of loss may intensify as adulthood gets closer. Build her life skills and confidence gradually by turning over more and more responsibility to her and helping her learn how to handle it.

- This year we'll set your curfew time with you. If that works, next year you can set your own time.

- Since you'll be taking driver's ed next summer, you can start pumping gas and checking the oil now.

Still allow her to express her fears or sense of loss. Just listen and let her process.

- I see.

- That sounds confusing.

- It sounds like you're excited and nervous at the same time.

Words and Phrases to Use

- We're here.

- Support

- It's normal.

- Sad

- Sometimes I miss the past.

- Future

- What do you imagine?

- Freedom

- Privileges

- Opportunities

What Not to Say and Do

Don't overromanticize childhood in how you talk about it. Don't say,

- You're so lucky to be a kid with no responsibilities.

- Kids have it so easy today.

- Being a parent is so much work.

Don't say or imply that adulthood is somehow a punishment. Don't say that her behavior now means that she won't be able to make it as an adult. Don't say,

- Just wait until you have to spend all day at a job you hate.

- How will you ever make a living?

- You'll never be able to take care of yourself at this rate.

Resources

Feel the Fear and Do It Anyway by Susan J. Jeffers. Fawcett, 1996.

Ready, Set, Grow! A What's Happening to My Body Book for Younger Girls by Lynda Madaras, illustrated by Linda Davick. Newmarket Press, 2003.

FEELINGS

"It's really hard for me when Mariella feels sad or angry; I feel so helpless. I want her to be happy, and I just want to cheer her up and distract her from those negative things. But now she just goes to her mom or stepmom to talk about those things, and I don't know what to do about it."—Maurizio

Things to Consider

A girl's awareness and acceptance of all her feelings is fundamental to her well-being. Little girls have feelings that come and go quickly as long as they can be openly expressed. When young, she needs your help to identify and put words to her feelings so she can recognize them. Her feelings are physical and real. Your acknowledgment of her feelings and their value is important to her developing understanding of how her experiences relate to the world outside herself.

As she gets older, she will start to feel the need to act more grown up and limit how she expresses her feelings. She may start to express many more negative than positive feelings at home, which often means that she's less able to express the negative emotions in other parts of her life. Don't take it personally; it's probably not about you, and in fact it means she knows that you'll still love her even if she's not feeling happy. This is a healthy transition as long as you help her realize that she can (and needs to) still feel a full range of feelings. The only thing that needs to change is the maturity of how she expresses them. In general, we need to be more concerned with helping our daughters express their true feelings than with how adultlike they can be in their expression.

Moms and dads face different challenges in helping a daughter with her feelings. Moms may tend to get too involved in a daughter's feelings, especially if they mirror feelings they had as girls. Dads may be totally mystified. On top of it, most men have learned to deny and repress feelings, and they feel worried and threatened by a daughter's strong emotions. Each parent will have different strengths in helping a daughter, too, so be a team and give her the best of each of your ways of coping.

What to Say and Do

1–7 YEARS OLD
Reward her for being direct about her feelings.

- I'm glad you told me how you feel.

- Feelings are a big part of us.

Help her recognize and put words to her feelings.

- You look like you're feeling sad. Tell me how you're feeling.

- You looked so proud when you rode your two-wheeler all the way down the driveway.

- I'm feeling angry and scared about my job.

8–13 YEARS OLD
Respond with empathy, understanding, and acceptance to all the feelings she expresses.

- I understand how you feel. I felt that way yesterday.

- That's a normal feeling. Everyone feels like that sometimes.

Ask her about her feelings every day in a calm, matter-of-fact way so she learns that talking about feelings is part of a relationship. Talk about your feelings the same way.

Show and tell her that she has the power to choose how to express her feelings when she knows what they are.

- You're feeling jealous that Tawnya won the prize. How do you want to handle that?

- I'm very disappointed that Uncle Shel canceled his visit at the last minute again. I'm figuring out how to talk with him about it so I don't sound defensive.

14 AND UP
Help her first feel her feelings and then apply reason to challenging situations. Show her how you do that.

- It sounds like you need to scream and throw some Nerf balls at the wall. Later let's talk about what you can do with the situation.

- I need a hug, This was a tough day and I'm not sure what to do.

Help her think out what she wants to do, but don't give advice unless directly asked.

- I see. How does that feel? What do you think?

- Where do your feelings and your plans come out on this?

Words and Phrases to Use

- Normal
- Okay
- Understand
- How about a hug?
- How are you feeling?

- Tell me about it.
- It looks like . . .
- Accept
- Human

What Not to Say and Do

Don't deny or contradict how she says she feels. Don't say,

- That's not how you really feel.

- Don't get scared; it's just pretend.

Don't overanalyze or overreact to certain feelings: that can give her the message those feelings are problems rather than normal parts of life.

Don't offer solutions in place of accepting and validating her feelings.

- No reason to be upset, We'll just find another team for you to join.

- Since Shelly is mean, I won't invite her to your party.

Words and Phrases to Avoid

- You don't feel that way.

- That's a bad feeling.

- You're crazy to feel that way.

- What's the matter with you?

- That's weird.

- That's negative.

- Just don't think about it.

- Have a cookie. That'll make you feel better.

Resources

How to Raise a Child with a High EQ: A Parents' Guide to Emotional Intelligence by Lawrence E. Shapiro. HarperCollins, 1998.

The Feelings Book: The Care and Keeping of Your Emotions by Lynda Madison, illustrated by Norm Bendell. Pleasant Company Publications, 2002.

My Feelings, Myself: A Growing Up Journal for Girls by Lynda and Area Madaras. Newmarket Press, 2002.

The Pathway by Laurel Mellin. HarperCollins, 2003.

Raising an Emotionally Intelligent Child by John Gottman. Simon & Schuster, 1998.

Today I Feel Silly and Other Moods That Make My Day by Jamie Lee Curtis, illustrated by Laura Cornell. HarperCollins, 1998.

FIXING AND BUILDING THINGS

"We've always gotten our daughter toys like Legos and building blocks, as well as dolls. But she never seemed interested in building or figuring out anything mechanical. Now that she's getting older, I want her to know how basic things work and how to construct and fix things herself so she won't be clueless. How can I get her interested in learning this stuff?"—Ray

Things to Consider

It's important to give your daughter a basic knowledge of mechanics and teach her how to use hand and power tools. Learning basic principles of geometry and physics by designing, building, and deconstructing things builds a comfort level for formal classes in high school. Equally important is developing her skill in troubleshooting—figuring out why something isn't working and how it might be fixed. These skills will help her be safe once she starts driving and will make everyday life much easier in other ways. She'll feel competent when she can help others and will be an informed consumer when she needs to get professional repairs or construction help.

Your example of interest and willingness to learn how to use tools and try building or repairing things is good for both of you. Time spent with Dad or Mom working on a joint project can be rewarding in and of itself, and seeing the final product is a constant reminder of what you've accomplished together.

What to Say and Do

1–7 YEARS OLD

Give her simple building and mechanical toys, including real hand tools that are sized for her. Encourage others to give these kinds of gifts. And play with her with them so she experiences the fun. Bring a social element into building and fixing things by including her friends and other family members. Include her as much as possible in any building or repairing you're doing, teaching her as you go. Set the situation up for success, teaching her the simplest things first and progressing as she gets more skilled.

- While Cecily is here, let's see what ideas she has for the tree house we're building.

- Here's the way to use the screwdriver. Now you try it.

- Can you help me measure this room to see how big a rug we want to get?

8–13 YEARS OLD

Take broken things apart together to explore how they are built and work.

- Look at how the pieces of this CD player fit together. It's fascinating.

- What do you think this part is for?

- The weather's warming up. Let's get your bike ready to ride by lubricating it and checking it over.

Encourage her creativity in designing and making things, even when the designs seem dubious. She'll learn so much from going through the process hands on, with your involvement and support, not your criticism. Be a team to solve the design/construction problems that come up.

- Hmm, this isn't working out to be as stable as we want. What do you think we should do now?

- How about rolling that heavy log up a board to get it on top since it's too heavy to lift?

Volunteer to work together on houses for Habitat for Humanity or similar projects.

14 AND UP
Give her responsibility for troubleshooting and repairing things on her own, with you as supportive observer.

- I'll be right here if you have any questions while you're rewiring your lamp.

- That home repair book we have will explain how to get your ring out of the sink trap.

Teach her the basics of car mechanics and maintenance before she gets her license: she'll be the most motivated then. Get her her own basic set of tools to use.

- Now that you're fifteen, here's your own personal copy of *Auto Repair for Dummies.*

- The tires look a little low, Please check them with the tire gauge and let me know if we need to add air.

Words and Phrases to Use

- We can do it together.
- Interesting
- I wonder
- How?

- What do you think?
- Let's try it.
- Experiment
- Fun

What Not to Say and Do

Don't criticize or take over her unskilled work when she's learning how to use tools and fix things.

- No, no, no! That's not how you do it.

- Just give me the hammer. I can do it faster and better.

Don't say or imply that boys and men are better with tools and mechanical things.

- Girls don't do that kind of thing. They hate to get their hands dirty.

- I can't fix that. Ask your uncle.

Words and Phrases to Avoid

- Can't

- Unmechanical

- Klutzy

- Shoddy work

Resources

Dare to Repair: A Do-It-Herself Guide to Fixing (Almost) Anything in the Home by Julie Sussman and Stephanie Glakas-Tenet. HarperCollins, 2002.

If It's Broke, Fix It! by Dan Ramsey and Judy Ramsey. Penguin, 2004.

The New Way Things Work by David Macauley. Houghton Mifflin, 1998.

Popular Mechanics for Kids book series, published by HarperCollins.

How Things Work: http://howthingswork.virginia.edu/home.html

How Stuff Works: www.howstuffworks.com/

FRIENDS

"Now that Gilda is in middle school, some of her friendships are changing and it's causing her grief. She made friends easily and could play with just about anyone. Now she's pickier and at the same time is upset if other girls don't include her. How long will this phase last and can I do anything to help?"—Marcus

Things to Consider

Starting around age seven, friends become particularly important to girls. Close relationships and connections are a key part of their psychological development. Girls look to friendships, especially with other girls, to help them understand themselves. And nearly every girl has times of friendship troubles during middle and high school. She's growing up and changing, and so are her friends. Sometimes those changes can cause painful endings to long-standing friendships.

Teach your daughter to be a kind and loyal friend. Teach her that if a "friend" treats her unkindly or disloyally, that person is not a true friend. Also teach her that sometimes friendships end, and that's for the best, even though it's difficult. Sometimes she might outgrow a friendship, and other times it will be her friend who gets distant. There's really no way to make those experiences easy for her. But she will survive them, and knowing she can talk to you about it is a huge help.

What to Say and Do

8–13 YEARS OLD
Be interested in her friends and friendships.

- What did you and Corinne do today?

- You and Helen have a lot of fun together.

Listen empathetically when she tells you about friendship troubles.

- That sounds really tough.

- It sounds like your feelings were hurt.

- You want to be kind to Nyesha, but you don't enjoy being with her as much as you used to.

Encourage her to talk about her concerns with her friends.

- It might be hard to bring it up, but if you don't talk about it, she'll never know how you feel.

14 AND UP
Make her friends very welcome at your house and show a genuine interest in them as people.

- You can bring your friends home anytime. Just give me a call first.

- Shaunte's family is fascinating. They've lived in so many places.

- When is Monica's next game? I want to go to it.

Understand her friendships will get more private as she gets older.

Encourage her to have boys as friends, not just romantic interests.

- It's neat that you and Des are friends. It gives you a different perspective on the whole girl-boy thing.

Words and Phrases to Use

- Loyalty
- Caring
- Honesty
- Buddies
- Like sisters

- Help each other.
- Support each other.
- Tell me about it.
- What do you think?

What Not to Say and Do

Don't criticize her friends or try to drive a wedge between them. Don't say,

- Why do you want to be friends with her?
- You have nothing in common.
- Her family isn't our type.

Don't intervene directly in her friendships. Don't say,

- I'm going to talk to her about what she said to you.

Words and Phrases to Avoid

- Drop her.
- She's mean.
- Don't worry about it.
- Friends are a dime a dozen.

Resources

Girlfighting: Betrayal and Rejection among Girls by Lyn Mikel Brown. New York University Press, 2003.

New Moon Friendship: Girls Write about Friends by the Girls Editorial Board, 2004 (for more information go to www.newmoon.org).

GIRL GROUPS

"My daughter is part of a couple of all-girl groups. Is it good for her to be in these groups? Or does she need to get more used to working with boys since that's what the real world is like?"—Maddie

Things to Consider

Being part of organized girl groups like Girl Scouts, Girls Incorporated, girls' sports teams, book groups, and service clubs is great for girls. A single-gender environment means that all the leaders will be girls and that girls will fill all the roles in whatever the group is doing. The experience of being a group leader and breaking out of traditional "girl stuff" has a proven positive influence on girls. This is especially valuable in the preteen and teen years, when girls get a lot of cultural pressure to defer to boys in mixed gender settings.

At the same time, girl groups can provide a place for girls to relate with less cliquey behavior than in more informal settings. Organized groups aren't immune to the effects of cliques, but the adults involved with the groups can be on the lookout for them and guide the group to deal with the problem directly. This helps girls learn ways to confront and lessen emotional aggression in other situations, too.

What to Say and Do

8–13 YEARS OLD
Ensure that your daughter belongs to at least one organized girls' group of her choice.

- Now that you're eight, you can join the YWCA with your own membership!
- I want you to give this group a try for two months. If it doesn't feel like it fits, then you can try a different one.

Talk with the adult leaders of her groups regularly so you know what's happening in the groups and they know what's happening with your girl.

Participate in the group when she asks you to and support her taking on leadership in the group.

- I'll help you start a book group with the girls from temple.

Encourage her to talk with you about her feelings about the group.

- I noticed that you haven't been talking about Girls' Circle much lately. What's been going on there?

14 AND UP
Strongly encourage her to stay involved in all-girl groups during her high school years.

- Your club is earning money for a trip to Guatemala. How exciting that will be!
- I know it's a little rough right now, but I hope you stay in the group and work it out. Is there any way I can help?

Words and Phrases to Use

- Friendship
- Leadership
- Sisterhood
- Girl stuff
- Fun
- Girl power

- Connecting
- Sharing

- Girls can do anything when they support each other.

What Not to Say and Do

Don't put down all-girl groups or discourage her from sticking with them. Don't say,

- Isn't it dorky to be a Girl Scout at your age?
- They just can't compete with the boys. That's why they have a girls' group.

Words and Phrases to Avoid

- That's just a gossip group.
- Girls' groups are wimpy.

Resources

Girls Club Kit: Start a Club and Find Friends, Fortune and Fun by Brooks Whitney, illustrated by Isabelle Dervaux. Pleasant Company Publications, 2002.

The Mother-Daughter Book Club by Shireen Dodson. Perennial, 1997.

Girl Scouts: www.gsusa.org

Girls Incorporated: www.girlsinc.org

Girls' Circle: http://drake.marin.k12.ca.us/stuwork/compapps/girlscircle/index.html

YWCA: www.ywca.org

GOALS, HOPES, AND DESIRES

"Amanda is full of crazy dreams and goals. There's no way they will all come true and I don't want her to be disappointed. Should I gently let her know that those things are beyond her grasp?"—Gabe

Things to Consider

Girls naturally have lots of dreams and goals for the future. Along with her hopes and desires they express her deepest self and give her motivation for learning and challenging herself. They inspire her to imagine herself rising beyond limitations and defying odds. These are all good things. Anyone who's had the experience of having even a small dream become reality knows how satisfying it is.

But as parents we understand the reality that some dreams may not come true, and we want to cushion the blow before it happens. But we shouldn't step in and tell her these dreams are impossible. Telling her to limit her dreams and goals cheats her of feeling that she can chart her own course.

Instead, we want to encourage our daughter to dream and set goals. We want her to hope and have desires. They are the energy that helps her persevere through difficulty and setbacks. We want to help her figure out how to take practical steps that can help make her dreams and goals a reality. We want her to feel the incredible feeling of imagining something and making it real by her own efforts. Even if she doesn't attain her biggest childhood dreams as an adult, it very often turns out that those dreams are directly related to the things that are most fulfilling to her later in life. And having dreams, goals, hopes, and desires enriches her life every day by expanding her vision and raising her sights.

What to Say and Do

1–7 YEARS OLD

Listen uncritically to her dreams and goals about the future.

- You want to be an explorer and discover new animals.
- You want to be a hero and save other people.

Be enthusiastic about her hopes and desires. Encourage her to talk about them.

- It's wonderful to dream of going to Mars some day!
- You love acting and want to be in plays more than anything.

8–13 YEARS OLD

Give her information and practical help in learning more and practicing skills that could help her goals to become real.

- Tell me about the story you wrote about time travel. You might be interested in this book about how time travel could work.
- Doctors start out by learning about sciences like biology and chemistry.
- You want to be a dancer. Taking three classes a week is a step toward that dream.

If some of her dreams get dashed, let her feel disappointed and then recover with your support.

- It feels very disappointing that you didn't get chosen for Space Camp.
- It's discouraging that there has never been a woman US president. But that

doesn't mean there never will be. What do you think it would take for a woman to get elected?

- No one in our family has finished college, but you can prove Grandpa wrong and be the first.

Around middle school some girls lose touch with their dreams and goals. They feel they shouldn't have any strong hopes or desires. Watch for this and find gentle ways to keep nurturing her dreams and goals. They are still inside her—they're just temporarily buried by the earthquake of puberty.

14 AND UP
She may express goals you think are meaningless—like becoming a celebrity or a millionaire. Let her have those goals and also explore other ones.

- I know you dream of being a celebrity. What are some of your other hopes?

- What do you wish the world were like?

Her ability to feel all kinds of desires and hopes is related to her being able to feel and accept her natural sexual desires. They aren't in separate compartments.

Words and Phrases to Use

- Dreams

- Reality

- Steps to your goal

- How can we try to make it happen?

- That didn't work. How about trying this?

- What will it take?

- Who can help?

What Not to Say and Do

Don't dismiss goals and dreams as worthless. Don't say:

- That will never happen.
- I told you to forget it.
- You're just a "pie in the sky" dreamer.
- None of my dreams ever came true.
- Hoping is a waste of time and energy.

Don't stifle her feelings of sexual desire with shame or guilt. Don't say:

- Good girls don't think about desire.
- Desire will just get you into trouble.

Words and Phrases to Avoid

- Totally impractical.
- Not worth thinking about.
- Dreams lead to disappointment.
- What's the point?
- Something always gets in the way of my dreams.

Resources

What Do You Really Want? How to Set a Goal and Go for It! A Guide for Teens by Beverly K. Bachel. Free Spirit Publishing, 2001.

HARASSMENT

"Emily just told us that a boy at school makes rude comments to her in the halls when there are no teachers around. She doesn't want us to make a big deal about it. She's not even sure the teacher will believe her because this boy is an A student. But we're furious and want it to stop. It's outrageous, and it's making her dislike school."—Jonathan

Things to Consider

Verbal and physical harassment intimidates girls and often affects their school performance and self-confidence. The school or organization (team, club, synagogue) is legally responsible for stopping any kind of harassment and providing a safe and respectful environment for everyone there. Even though your daughter might not want you to intervene, this is a situation when you need to if she's not able to go to the teacher or leader herself. Offer to help her practice how she will talk to the responsible adult and offer to go with her. If she chooses not to do that, tell her that it's your responsibility to take action yourself.

What to Say and Do

8 AND UP

Teach her what harassment is and that it's never OK.

- No one can touch you without your OK.

- It's wrong when kids say bad things to or about another kid. If anyone does, tell me about it.

- The school is in charge of stopping harassment. You don't have to do it by yourself.

- It sounds like Jason is being harassed. That's wrong.

Show her that you take it seriously and will take action with her or on your own.

- We need to talk to the principal about this. Do you want to do it? I'll go with you if you like.

- It's OK that you don't want to talk to the minister about it. I'll talk to her.

Understand that she may feel guilty or ashamed that this is happening.

Reassure her it's not her fault or responsibility.

Words and Phrases to Use

- Everyone deserves respect.

- Harassment is wrong.

- It doesn't matter why they did it.

- I'm sorry this happened.

- It can feel scary.

- It's illegal.

- We need to talk to someone.

What Not to Say and Do

Don't imply she caused the harassment. Don't say,

- What did you do to make him say that?
- Did you get her mad?

Don't let it drop without going to the responsible adults. Don't say,

- OK, I won't talk to the principal since you're embarrassed.

Words and Phrases to Avoid

- Victim
- Cause
- Reason
- Just ignore it.
- Don't let it get to you.

Resources

And Words Can Hurt Forever: How to Protect Adolescents from Bullying, Harassment, and Emotional Violence by James Garbarino and Ellen Delara. Simon & Schuster, 2003.

American Association of University Women: www.aauw.org (legal rights and what parents and students can do about harassment)

Harassment-Free Hallways: How to Stop Sexual Harassment in School: www.aauw.org/k-12/ (found on the AAUW home page)

HEALTHY TOUCH

"My fifteen-year-old, Lynette, won't accept a hug from anyone in the family, especially me. On the other hand, I'm a little uneasy with how readily my six-year-old, Missy, will leap into the lap of a relative or family friend she hardly knows. I worry that Missy is completely indiscriminate about that, but I also don't want to crush her spirit about it, either."—Henry

Things to Consider

When it comes to their bodies, girls face very complex issues. In the media, girls' bodies are regularly objectified and sexualized. Culture and family often tell girls that they face great risk of physical violation. In response, girls have the need to command their personal space. But they also place great importance on the connection of relationships. They may go back and forth in an emotional and psychological tug-of-war with their need for both connection and independence.

Healthy touch:

- Comforts and supports her
- Affirms her as a person
- Respects and is sensitive to her personal likes and dislikes

- Is given at her request or with her free permission

- Helps her feel strong, lovable, and able to delight in herself

What to Say and Do

AGE 1–7

Explain matter-of-factly about bad and good touch. Help her recognize and trust her own feelings.

- The only people allowed to touch you there are you, Mom or Dad when we're bathing you, or the doctor when she's checking you.

- I see you feel relaxed and comforted when I rub your back.

Support her being in control of her body and touch she wants. Tell her what to do if she gets touched in a way she doesn't want. Teach her to respect other people's limits.

- You don't have to hug Aunt Mary. You can say no thank you.

- You don't like it when Katie babysits? Tell me about it.

- I love to tickle and horse around with you, but when you say "Stop," I always will.

AGE 8–13

She will want more privacy as she gets older. She may want privacy from Dad sooner than Mom. Be sensitive to this and respect it. Issues of touch with peers will start to arise.

- Tell Nick you don't want him to pinch you. Tell the teacher if he keeps doing it.

- You can put on your bathing suit in the bathroom.

AGE 14 AND UP

Teen girls are becoming aware of their sexual desire and have contradictory feelings about the kind of touch they do and don't want from family and in romances. Media messages about appropriate sexual touch for teen girls are very confusing and very influential. She may feel she needs to let dates touch her in ways she doesn't like. Support her in trusting her own feelings about what's healthy for her.

- If you love someone and they love you, you will be able to talk about what kind of touching is OK with you.

- Kissing, cuddling, and sex can be wonderful when you feel safe and it's truly your choice.

- You don't ever have to say yes to touching that you don't want.

- It's your right to change your mind at any time about what touching is OK with you.

Words, Phrases, and Actions to Use

- It's up to you.

- When her bedroom door is closed, knock and ask if you can come in.

- I believe you.

- I understand.

- Stop immediately if she says no about any kind of touch.

- You're in charge.

- Tell me whenever you feel uncomfortable.

- Moms, show her that you are comfortable with your own body, letting her see you nude if she's okay with that.

What Not to Say and Do

Don't encourage her to do or allow things to others she wouldn't want. Don't say,

- If she pushes you just push her back.

- When your brother says stop tickling he doesn't really mean it.

Don't encourage her to swallow her discomfort. Don't say,

- What's the big deal—it was just a little hug.

Don't act as though a teenager's interest in sexual touch is wrong. Don't say,

- What's the matter with you? Only a cheap girl would do that.

- If you want a boyfriend, you're going to have to do the gross things boys want.

Words, Phrases, and Actions to Avoid

- Don't hit, slap, or spank her.

- You HAVE to kiss Uncle John or his feelings will be hurt.

- It's nothing—just forget it.

- Why are you such a cold fish?

Resources

Deal With It: A Whole New Approach to Your Body, Brain and Life as a gURL by Esther Drill, Rebecca Odes, Heather McDonald. Pocket, 1999.

www.goodtouchbadtouch.com

ILLNESS

"A boy in my daughter's class has cancer. She's very upset about it and is having nightmares. Some days she doesn't want to go to school. She's taking this very hard. How can we help her with it?"—César

Things to Consider

When a family member or peer or your daughter herself is seriously ill, it's a stressful time for all of you. Her concern and uncertainty may overwhelm her at times. She may develop fears that seem unreasonable or illogical. Share the facts with her simply and sensitively, accept her feelings, and reassure her that adults are taking care of the situation as best they can. Try to keep her routine normal, but allow her to opt out of some activities for a while if she wants to. Do things together that you know help her relieve stress.

What to Say and Do

1–7 YEARS OLD
Hugs and physical comfort are key at this age. Keep explanations simple and basic.

- Uncle John is sick and the doctors are helping him.

- Give me a hug.

- Let's sit in the rocking chair and read a book.

8 AND UP
Give her information as she can handle it. Be sensitive to her individual ability to cope.

- I heard that Kyesha has leukemia. Do you want to know more about it?

- Because of the medicine that fights the cancer, she lost her hair. It will grow back later.

Encourage her to express her sadness, anger, fear—whatever feelings she has.

- If you have a bad dream, you can come talk with us about it right away.

- It's good to cry. I feel sad, too.

- It's difficult to understand why you got sick and not someone else. Sometimes it just happens.

- Would it help to say a prayer?

Words and Phrases to Use

- You can tell me anything.

- You can ask me anything.

- I'll tell you the truth.

- The doctors are doing what they can.

- The doctors are very good.

What Not to Say and Do

Don't contradict her feelings. Don't say,

- It doesn't help for you to get upset.

- Why should you be scared? You're not the one who's sick.

- Don't waste your tears.

Don't refuse to answer her questions. Don't say,

- You don't want to know about that.

- It's too hard to talk about.

- That won't change anything.

Words and Phrases to Avoid

- Why us?

- Catastrophe

- Hopeless

- It's his own fault.

- She deserves it.

- If you're bad, you might get sick.

Resources

Germs Make Me Sick! by Melvin Berger, illustrated by Marylin Hafner. HarperCollins, 1995.

Healing Images for Children: Teaching Relaxation and Guided Imagery to Children Facing Cancer and Other Serious Illnesses by Nancy C. Klein. Inner Coaching, 2001.

Girl Power: www.girlpower.gov (a great resource on girls' health for both girls and parents)

IEmily.com: www.iemily.com (website for girls about a wide range of health issues)

INDEPENDENCE

"Brittany wants more independence than I think she's ready for. I know she needs to learn how to handle things for herself, but she's only twelve and her judgment isn't always the best. How do we know how much latitude to give her?"—Pete

Things to Consider

Parents seem to have an intuitive desire to shelter and protect daughters more than sons. We feel that they're more vulnerable and not as safe out in the world. Even though we might not want to admit it, emotionally many of us wouldn't mind going back to the times when girls didn't venture out on their own. But it's the twenty-first century and girls want to be full participants in the world. And even if it makes us somewhat anxious, it also makes us very proud to see them growing up and facing challenges with confidence and savvy.

Fostering age-appropriate independence is important to our daughters' development. It gives them the skills to ultimately succeed as adults and take full responsibility for themselves. With this in mind, we need to take their current judgment and skills into account as we gradually give them more independence. It's just as harmful to overwhelm them with too much independence too early as it is to keep them sheltered too long.

What to Say and Do

1–7 YEARS OLD
Foster a girl's independence within safe boundaries you create.

- You can do that all by yourself!

- What a big girl you are.

- You did a good job on that.

8–13 YEARS OLD
School and activities help her develop independence.

- You're learning so much.

- Now you can walk to school by yourself.

Ask her what she wants and give positive feedback when she makes independent choices.

- Choosing the trumpet instead of the flute showed your independence.

- You love fencing so much, it doesn't matter that none of your friends do it.

- It's great how you read the recipe and cooked it yourself! It smells delicious.

14 AND UP
Give her as much independence as you feel she can handle. Sometimes, give her just a little more than you're sure she's ready for to let her test her abilities.

- You can manage your homework on your own. I'm going to stop asking you if it's done.

- I think you know for yourself if a certain party will be within our rules.

- We want to try giving you no curfew. We think you're ready to handle it.

Words and Phrases to Use

- Independent

- By yourself

- You know what to do.

- You can handle it.

- I trust you.

- You're growing up.

What Not to Say and Do

Don't keep her inappropriately dependent. Don't say,

- A girl can't do that by herself.

- You need me to help you.

- I knew you couldn't handle it.

Words and Phrases to Avoid

- Irresponsible

- Immature

- It's not totally safe.

- Absolutely not.

- You can't go away to camp (or college).

Resources

Declarations of Independence: Empowered Girls in Young Adult Literature, 1990–2001 by Joanne Brown and Nancy St. Clair. Rowman & Littlefield, 2002.

The It's My Life Book by Nancy Rue. Zonderkidz, 2001.

Strong, Smart, & Bold: Empowering Girls for Life by Carla Fine. Foreword by Jane Fonda. HarperCollins, 2001.

INTERNET

"I hear horror stories of girls being lured by perverts in chat rooms, and then them being assaulted or manipulated. Plus, there's so much porn and other garbage online. I'm tempted to ban my daughter from using the Internet."
—Phil

Things to Consider

Research shows a complex picture about how the Internet affects a child's life. For example, in 1999, the Kaiser Family Foundation found that children who use a computer for enjoyment for more than an hour a day watch about one hour and forty minutes more TV a day than children who don't use computers at all, but they also read about twenty-two minutes more a day. In other words, kids who spend more time using a computer usually spend more time watching TV, but also spend more time reading.

For girls, the Internet, e-mail, chat rooms, and instant messages (IMs) can be ways to connect, communicate, and build a virtual community with other kids. But those same tools can facilitate cruel gossip and bullying, online predation, and a flood of marketing fed to girls. Less than half of parents use Internet blocking devices and/or monitor a child's Internet activity.

It's very important to monitor her online usage, so keep the computer in a common area of the house, tell your kids that you will regularly examine their e-mail messages and chat rooms, and have them sign an Internet safety agreement that you draw up together. This helps them set better limits for themselves and use you as "the bad cop" if online friends complain.

What to Say and Do

1–7 YEARS OLD
Children this age should not spend any time online without direct adult supervision.

8 AND UP
Follow the National Institute on Media and the Family's guidelines for child Internet use, review it with your daughter often, and consider drawing it up as a contract you sign with each other.

- **People you meet on the Internet are strangers.** Just as your children should not give out their address, telephone number, name, location of school, or any other information to a stranger, they should not give out personal information to people they meet on the Internet.

- **Talk with children about what they are seeing and doing on the Internet.** Encourage your children to talk to you right away about anything on the Internet that makes them feel uncomfortable.

- **Ask your children about the people they meet on the Internet.** Make sure that your children talk to you directly about anyone they have met on the Internet who wants to meet them in person.

- **Meeting "friends" from the Internet in person requires adult supervision.** Establish a firm rule with your children that they may not meet someone they know from the Internet unless a parent or other responsible adult goes with them.

- **E-mailing personal information should only be done with permission.** Explain to your children that it is not safe to e-mail a picture of themselves or anything else without first checking with you. Let them know that just as it is important that you know who their friends are and what they are doing with them, it is important that they talk with you before beginning an e-mail friendship with a new person.

- **Have frequent discussions with your child about conversations and messages they are receiving through the Internet.** Encourage your children to talk to you about any messages that are mean or make them feel uncomfortable in any way. Reassure them that it is not their fault if they get a message of that kind. Urge them to confide in you, reminding them that you are "on their team."

- **Set clear "house rules" around use of the Internet.** As with all media, set limits around the use of the Internet. Be clear about your rules and expectations, and let them know that you want them to enjoy the wonderful resource the Internet is. Emphasize that the guidelines you have set up will enable them to enjoy the Internet safely.

(Source: www.mediafamily.org/facts/tips_surfsafe.shtml)

Words and Phrases to Use

- You can tell me anything about what happens online, and we can discuss and work on it calmly together.

- Think of the Internet as a neighborhood; only do, say, or tolerate something there that you would do, say, or tolerate down the street.

- Like in our neighborhood, you don't have the expectation of total privacy, and I am free to observe what you are doing.

What Not to Say and Do

Kids often know more about the Internet and computers than adults, so be careful how much freedom you give her. Don't say,

- Sure, you can set up the blocking software yourself.

Don't downplay the Internet. Don't say,

- I don't want to know what goes on in your chat rooms.

- Who cares if Sally said something mean about you online. It's only the Internet.

Resources

Dr. Dave's Cyberhood: Making Media Choices That Create a Healthy Electronic Environment for Your Kids by David Walsh, PhD, Founder of the National Institute on Media and the Family. Fireside, 2001.

Parent's Guide to Protecting Children in Cyberspace by Parry Aftab. McGraw-Hill, 2002.

Kaiser Family Foundation: Kids and Media and the New Millennium: www.kff.org/content/1999/1535/

Center for Media Education, 1511 K Street, NW, Suite 518, Washington, DC 20005. Phone: (202) 628-2620. www.cme.org

Tech-Savvy: Educating Girls in the New Computer Age: www.aauw.org/k-12/

LEADERSHIP

*"Marissa is a natural leader, and my other daughter Sharmay is more of a fol-
lower. But they're both smart. People give Marissa a lot of praise and attention,
and I feel that Sally gets a bit neglected and lost. How can I get Sally to be more
of a leader; I know she has it in her."—Denise*

Things to Consider

Most of us would like to think of our daughters as leaders; being a follower doesn't
sound very successful. But both leaders and followers play an important role in making
society work. Your daughter may well be a follower in some situations and a leader in
others. It's very healthy for her to have the flexibility and self-confidence to do either,
depending on what she wants and what the situation calls her to do.

There are certain personalities that are more obvious as leaders, and if your
daughter has that personality, you may see it from an early age. But remember that
there are many ways of leading, and the identified leader is rarely the only leader in a
situation. Usually, less visible, informal leaders also exist, and their roles are just as
important. The key to true leadership is a focus on being of real service both to yourself and to others. That's why being a good follower can also be a form of leadership.

What to Say and Do

8–13 YEARS OLD

Help her see how she's a leader and a follower in various ways. Value both roles.

- You were a leader when you volunteered to be a crossing guard.

- The way you helped with Meg's campaign for class president was really important.

Identify leadership with her special qualities and gifts and how they serve her and others.

- You were a leader for the team when you showed Jesse your jump shot and then helped him practice his own way.

- The friendly way you treat new kids in the drama club makes it a better group.

14 AND UP

Acknowledge that leadership can be difficult if her stand is not popular. Encourage her when needed.

- You were a courageous leader when you talked to the principal about that teacher being unfair to other kids, even though she didn't agree with what you thought.

Emphasize the inner satisfaction of leading and following/supporting as needed and suited to her talents.

- It must feel great to be captain of the team that improved so much even though you didn't make the playoffs.

- Watching your orchestra, I could see how proud you were of the soloist.

Words and Phrases to Use

- Leadership
- Support
- Responsibility
- Service
- The good of the group

- Conviction
- Beliefs
- Goals
- Your niche
- How your talents fit in

What Not to Say and Do

Don't box her into thinking of herself as only a follower or only a leader. Don't say,

- Why aren't you the captain? You're the best player.
- You'll always be back in the crowd and not out front.

Words and Phrases to Avoid

- She's just a follower.
- There can only be one leader.
- There's only one way.

Resources

Closing the Leadership Gap: Why Women Can and Must Help Run the World by Marie C. Wilson. Viking, 2004.

Female Advantage: Women's Ways of Leadership by Sally Helgesen. Doubleday, 1995.

Hesselbein on Leadership by Frances Hesselbein. John Wiley & Sons, 2002.

Leadership the Eleanor Roosevelt Way by Robin Gerber. Portfolio, 2003.

LOVE AND COMPASSION

"Jenny is loving and compassionate sometimes. Other times she's very self-centered and childish. I want to help her develop her compassion more."
—Chris

Things to Consider

It's wonderful to see our daughters care for other people and be kind. We wish they were like that all the time. But are adults loving and compassionate all the time? It's unlikely. As a child, it's normal for her to be self-centered and childish much of the time.

It's also important to remember that girls are socialized to care about others, sometimes more than themselves. That's not healthy, and we want to be aware of not imposing that kind of self-effacement. That said, we can definitely encourage her feelings and acts of love and compassion for others by acting that way ourselves and recognizing her when she does.

What to Say and Do

1–7 YEARS OLD

Treat her with love and compassion. Mention it when you see her treating others that way.

- I saw you help your little brother when he fell down. That was kind.

- Is that something I can help with?

- You're a loving person.

8–13 YEARS OLD

Give her ways to extend her compassion beyond people she knows personally.

- Collecting for UNICEF on Halloween helps children all over the world get health care.

- Reading about how girls are treated in Afghanistan upset you. Let's think of how we can do something to help.

14 AND UP

Her love and compassion now may show itself as activism. Support that.

- You care a lot about justice for the poor and I support that.

- I'm proud that you think of other people and their welfare along with your own.

Words and Phrases to Use

- Love

- Compassion

- Caring

- Justice

- Grateful

- Fortunate

- Understanding

- Reaching out

- Helping

- Connecting

What Not to Say and Do

Don't expect her to act like a saint. Don't say,

- You say you care about others but you're selfish.

- You're loving sometimes, but you should be that way all the time.

- Why do you always think about yourself first?

- You should feel terrible about that.

Don't pooh-pooh the value of love and compassion. Don't say,

- It's a joke. Everyone just looks out for themselves.

- Don't be a sap.

- Why should you care? It doesn't affect our family.

Words and Phrases to Avoid

- Selfish

- Inconsiderate

- Not caring

- It won't help.

- It's too big a problem.

- Don't be naïve.

- You can't make a difference.

Resources

Growing Good Kids: 28 Activities to Enhance Self-Awareness, Compassion, and Leadership by Deb Delisle. Free Spirit Publishing, 1997.

Lovingkindness: The Revolutionary Art of Happiness by Sharon Salzberg. Random House, 2002.

MENTORS

"I'd like for my daughter to have a mentor, but since she's not 'at risk' she doesn't qualify for any mentor programs."—Peggy

Things to Consider

Mentors are great for girls as they move into the larger world from the family. Most of us have had informal mentors ourselves, even though we might not call them that. Just because your daughter's not in a mentor program doesn't mean she can't have a mentor. In fact, she might have one or more right now, if you think about it creatively. Her mentor could be her music or religion teacher, a favorite babysitter, an older cousin, a coach, a librarian, or any number of other people she interacts with.

A mentor is often someone with whom she has a long-term relationship, but it can also be someone she's met only a couple times. What makes someone her mentor is her feeling that they know, support, and value her for who she really is. At the same time, they help her learn how to stay true to herself and her values as she makes her way in the world. Her mentor will help correct her if she gets off course or teach her specific skills that she needs to reach her personal goals. A mentor is always in her corner, no matter what.

What to Say and Do

8–13 YEARS OLD
Provide opportunities for her to find formal or informal mentors.

- You really like the choir director and value her opinion.

- Your basketball coach has taught you a lot about your strengths.

Encourage her to listen to and talk things over with adults other than you.

- I think it would help you make up your mind to talk with the youth director.

- When he gave you that feedback, he showed how much he thinks of your potential.

14 AND UP
Encourage her to provide mentoring to younger kids if she's interested.

- You've gotten so good at pottery they'd love to have you help with the beginners.

- The Y is looking for high school kids to help coach swimming.

Realize that her ability to get support from nonfamily adults is valuable.

- I'm glad you can talk with your dance teacher about private things.

- Having different people to talk with gives you lots of perspectives.

Words and Phrases to Use

- Mentor
- Friend
- Guidance
- Inspiration
- Support
- Teaching
- Coaching

What Not to Say and Do

Don't act jealous of her mentors. Don't say,

- Why do you listen to the coach, but if I said that you'd ignore it?
- I'm just your mom. Go ahead and forget about me.

Don't ignore it if a "mentor" seems to be manipulating her. Trust your instincts.

Words and Phrases to Avoid

- You have to choose between loyalty to our family and that coach.
- You don't need a mentor. There's nothing wrong with you.
- Why do you care what she thinks?
- Don't you have your own mind?
- Mentors are for troubled kids.

Resources

For All Our Daughters: How Mentoring Helps Young Women and Girls Master the Art of Growing Up by Pegine Echevarria. Chandler House Press, 1998.

MISTAKES

"Tanaka hates to make mistakes, which makes her an easy kid. She doesn't want to do anything wrong, and we hardly ever have to discipline her. But I wonder if her fear of mistakes is unhealthy in a young girl."—Suki

Things to Consider

The kinds of mistakes most girls make may seem minor to us as parents, but the mistakes feel huge to them. A girl may try to avoid making mistakes in order to please you. But no one can avoid all mistakes, and at these times our daughters will need resiliency. Being able to make mistakes and recover from them is an essential skill for a fulfilling life.

A girl will learn a lot about mistakes and resiliency from your response to her mistakes and your own, too. By taking our mistakes in stride and learning from them ourselves, we can equip her to do the same. As she gets older, having made mistakes will help her think ahead about possible consequences and make better choices.

What to Say and Do

1–7 YEARS OLD
Show her that mistakes are normal and can usually be fixed.

- Oops, it spilled. That's OK. Let's get a towel and clean it up.

- It was a mistake. You didn't mean to hurt Stacy. Give her a hug and say you're sorry.

When a mistake can't be fixed, share your feelings and also let her know she's still OK.

- The lamp broke in so many pieces we can't fix it. I'm sad but I still love you.

8–13 YEARS OLD

Help her figure out how to learn from mistakes without taking them personally.

- When you lost the part after not memorizing the lines, you learned something important about being in a play.

- Getting a D on that paper you wrote in English was hard, but you decided you wouldn't do that again, so it was a good thing.

If she takes mistakes more in stride than you do, let her do it her way and learn from her.

- When Rosie used your scooter and crashed it by mistake, I learned from you that her friendship was more important than a thing. I'm going to remember that.

14 AND UP

By this age, you want her to feel completely responsible for her mistakes and how she copes with them. Offer support if she's too hard on herself, but don't intervene in logical consequences.

- It was really tough to have Allie stop being your friend when you passed those notes about her. I can understand how both of you felt. Maybe she'll forgive you in a while.

- I think it's OK that you got some wrong answers on the social studies test. I know you studied hard. What would help you feel better about it?

Teach her how to forgive herself and others for mistakes.

- I know it hurt when Rajiv didn't call after your date. You were forgiving when he said he was sorry.

- You wish you hadn't had that accident, but I appreciate that you were honest about driving too fast. We forgive you, and now that you're paying for the increased insurance and promised us you won't drive so fast again, it's time to forgive yourself.

Words and Phrases to Use

- Oops.
- Mistakes happen.
- How can you make it better?
- I know you didn't mean it.

- You're still a good person.
- I love you.
- Forgive
- Accept

What Not to Say and Do

Don't try to prevent her from ever making a mistake. Don't say,

- Why try? It might not work.
- It'll probably be a disaster.
- It would be awful if something goes wrong.

Don't shield her from appropriate, logical consequences of her mistakes. Don't say,

- It doesn't matter that your bike is lost; we'll get another tomorrow.

Words and Phrases to Avoid

- Awful
- It's your fault.

- Blame

- You should have known.

- Where's your head?

Resources

Doing It Right the First Time: A Short Guide to Learning from Your Most Memorable Errors, Mistakes, and Blunders by Gerard I. Nierenberg. John Wiley & Sons, 1996.

MONEY

"Sometimes Yolanda acts like we're her own personal bank, with unlimited funds. Money was scarce when I was growing up, and I admit that now I don't want to deny her anything. I feel proud that we can get her everything she wants, even if it stretches us a little thin. But I know this attitude isn't good for her in the long run."—Tracy

Things to Consider

Managing money well is a skill few adults have, so it's no surprise that even fewer girls have it. This is one area where we need to get our own house in order before we can expect our daughters to adopt better habits. We don't have to be perfect, but we need to honestly examine our own feelings, attitudes, and values about money and decide which ones we want to pass on to our girls. Then we need to do everything we can to change our habits that conflict with what we want to teach them.

Living within our means and making active choices about how to do that is the most useful thing we can teach her about managing money. This is true whether we have a lot or a little. Have a family budget that you're all in on, and let her know how the family's money is spent. Bringing the reality out in the open demystifies the whole thing, sharpens your focus if needed, and gives her valuable skills for the future.

Make sure she sees both Mom and Dad making financial decisions. When you feel she's ready (ten is a good age), give her a weekly or monthly budget (different than an allowance) of her own to manage for specific expenses like school lunches, clothes, gifts, and entertainment. Let her control it, even if she runs out before the end of the month. And don't bail her out if she runs out. If that happens a few times, she'll soon learn to pace her spending and start comparing price to value.

Once she has mastered that, get her a checking account (it will probably have to be a joint account with a parent until she's eighteen) with a debit card so she can learn the mechanics of balancing the account each month. Around age twelve, introduce her to investing through savings bonds, CDs, and mutual funds in her name (the amount invested is not as important as the experience). Show her how you or other family members are investing for long-term goals like a house, her future education, and your retirement, and how the quarterly statements show growth or loss. Help her understand the difference between saving and investing. In learning to manage money, nothing can take the place of actual experience doing it while she's still under your guidance and supervision.

What to Say and Do

8–13 YEARS OLD
Create limits on how your family spends money and be open about them. Talk about choices and options.

- Our movie budget is twenty-five dollars a month and we've already spent that. We can play a card game or take a walk in the park today.

- We can eat out once a week or skip this week and go twice next week. What would you rather do?

- We give three hundred dollars a month to charity, including synagogue. Help us decide how much to give to which groups.

Gradually give her increasing responsibility for handling the parts of the family budget that relate directly to her. Teach her how to balance a bank statement.

- Your clothing budget is seventy-five dollars a month this year.

- It didn't balance because you wrote the wrong amount for this check in the register. That's why the account got overdrawn. It helps to write the check amount down when you write the check.

14 AND UP

Turn over all responsibility (except for the total amount) for her daily expenses to her management. Be willing to negotiate if she makes a logical case for a different amount, but don't bail her out for lack of planning.

- We think you're ready to handle this, so we're giving you two hundred dollars a month to cover all your regular expenses.

- By showing us how you spent your money the last two months, you convinced us to increase your budget.

If possible, give her a set amount of money to invest a few times a year and let her decide where to invest it.

When she starts thinking about college, include the financial realities of what you can afford in your discussions.

Words and Phrases to Use

- Managing
- Planning
- Budget
- Choices
- Trade-offs
- Value
- Smart shopping
- Generosity

- Giving
- Sharing
- Balancing
- Money is a tool.
- I'm grateful for what we have.
- What we have is what we need.
- We're fortunate.

What Not to Say and Do

Don't keep the family's financial status a mystery from her. Don't say,

- You don't need to know how much money we have.

- Just believe me that we can't afford it.

Don't say one thing and do another.

- You have to save half your allowance and not a penny less.

- I earn the money, so I can spend it however I want.

Words and Phrases to Avoid

- If only we were rich.

- Money would solve everything.

Actions to Avoid

- Don't spend beyond your means.

- Avoid not planning for the future.

- Avoid not investing.

Resources

Consuming Kids: The Hostile Takeover of Childhood by Susan Linn. The New Press, 2004.

Living Simply With Children: A Voluntary Simplicity Guide for Moms, Dads, and Kids Who Want to Reclaim the Bliss of Childhood and the Joy of Parenting by Marie Sherlock (Three Rivers, 2003)

Material World: A Global Family Portrait by Peter Menzel. Sierra Club Books, 1995.

New Moon Money: How to Get It, Spend It, and Save It by the Girls Editorial Board. Crown Publishing, 2000.

Prince Charming Isn't Coming: How Women Get Smart about Money by Barbara Stanny. Penguin, 1999.

Raising Financially Fit Kids by Joline Godfrey. Ten Speed Press, 2004.

Selling Out America's Children: How America Puts Profits Before Values and What Parents Can Do by David Walsh, PhD (Fairview Press, 1996)

National Association of Investors Clubs Teen Guide to Investing: www.nais.org

MORALITY

"We've taught Sophie our values, but how do we know if she'll live by them?"—Deion

Things to Consider

Every family lives by values and morals, but we don't all define them the same way. What are parents to do?

Most importantly, we need to live by our own morals, whatever they are. Preaching to our daughter will not have a lasting effect if we don't "walk the talk" ourselves. It helps to tell her what values you feel are open to discussion and which are not. When she's a teen, expect her to explore her values and challenge your moral beliefs from time to time. Listen with an open mind, and change your mind if she persuades you to see it her way. She needs to think through what she believes and come to the morality that she will live by. We parents can make this process very difficult if we say that any deviation from our values is wrong. We have to decide if sharing certain beliefs is more important than our relationship with her.

What to Say and Do

1–7 YEARS OLD
Share your values in daily life.

- Every time we shop, you can pick out one item for the food shelf.

- Saying grace before we eat is important.

8–13 YEARS OLD
Recognize it when she acts on her values.

- You were kind to put your quarter in the collection box.

- It's generous to give one of your favorite toys to the shelter.

Talk about values you see other people living.

- The Joneses have only one car because they value clean air more than convenience.

- I liked hearing about the kids who found a wallet and returned it.

14 AND UP
Let your values and morality be up for thoughtful discussion with mutual respect.

- I'd like to hear what you believe about the death penalty.

- I don't agree about that but I respect your beliefs.

- I never thought about it that way. I'm going to think about it some more.

Encourage her to question and explore her values.

- What do you think is behind that belief?

- Did you look at it from this perspective?

Words and Phrases to Use

- Respect

- Personal

- Strength

- Actions speak louder than words.

What Not to Say and Do

Don't categorically refuse to discuss values with her. Don't say,

- That's immoral and I don't want to talk about it.

- What do you know?

Don't make fun of her moral decisions. Don't say,

- She thinks she can save the world by not eating meat.

- Why are you making such a big deal about it?

Words and Phrases to Avoid

- Who cares what you think?

- I know what's right.

- Don't you dare tell me I'm wrong.

Resources

Building Moral Intelligence: The Seven Essential Virtues That Teach Kids to Do the Right Thing by Michele D. Borba. John Wiley & Sons, 2002.

10-Minute Life Lessons for Kids: 52 Fun and Simple Games and Activities to Teach Your Child Honesty, Trust, Love, and Other Important Values by Jamie C. Miller. Harper-Collins, 1998.

MOVING

"I've been offered a wonderful job several states away. My wife and I are very excited about the opportunity, but we have some mixed feelings. We fear it will be hard for Zandra since she's in middle school and her friends are so important right now. Should we consider passing up this chance to move?"
—Dominic

Things to Consider

A move can be a positive, negative, or mixed experience at practically any age, adult or kid. Generally, the older your daughter is, the more she may resist a move. Even if she doesn't want to move, if she gets the support she needs from you, she will be able to adjust and be happy as time passes. It can be an opportunity for a new start, exploring new interests and making new friends. In a society as mobile as ours, knowing she can move and make a good life in a new place is a good thing for her to learn.

You can help her adjust as smoothly as possible by involving her in decisions and details of the move. Taking her to the new community before the move gives her an image of her new home and dispels fears. Planning ahead for her new school, teams, and other key activities is important. Most of all, let her feel sad about leaving her current home and friends. Help her stay in touch with them if she wants to. Let her follow her own timetable in embracing her new life. Trust that she can adjust and she will, with your support.

What to Say and Do

1–7 YEARS OLD

Tell her about the move when you start making plans so she doesn't feel insecure about what's happening.

Have a good-bye gathering with friends and ask them to give her a small thing to take along.

Emphasize what is not going to change.

- You'll have your same bed and toys in the new apartment.
- We're all going together.

8–13 YEARS OLD

Tell her as much as possible about her new school, teachers, and so on, and give her some control over new things.

- Here's a picture of the school and your classroom. You'll take a bus like you do now.
- You can arrange things in your new bedroom however you want.
- You can take an instrument in the new school. What do you want it to be?

Accept her feelings of loss, anger, and fear of the unknown.

- It's sad to say good-bye to friends you've known for your whole life. It's OK to cry.
- I know you feel angry about moving and that's all right.

14 AND UP

Expect her to be a bit self-centered about how the move will affect her.

Make it easy to stay in touch with old friends.

- We'll have e-mail, and we can come back in the summer to visit.

- Laurel and her family say they'll drive out to see us for spring break.

Welcome her new friends.

- I'm glad you invited Shirley to come over. I like her.

- Would your friends like to stay for dinner?

- I can drive you all to the movies on Friday.

Words and Phrases to Use

- Good friends
- New friends
- Opportunities
- Feelings

- Miss them
- I understand.
- Thanks for helping.

What Not to Say and Do

Don't move unless you think it's going to be positive for the family in the long run.

Don't deny that moving can be stressful. Don't say,

- Don't look so glum. It's much better than this town.

- You don't have anything to complain about.

Don't downplay or overplay the challenges. Don't say,

- Don't expect to find a friend as good as Gracia there.

- You'll be fine; you'll make new friends easily.

Words and Phrases to Avoid

- You're so spoiled.

- You only think about yourself.

- I had to move every two years when I was a kid, and I survived.

- We don't have a choice.

Resources

My Best Friend Moved Away by Nancy Carlson. Puffin, 2003.

Let's Talk about Moving to a New Place by Diana S. Helmer. Rosen Publishing, 2003.

NICENESS

"I want Tamika to act nice and have good manners. Sometimes I think she's sassy just to embarrass me. How can I get her to be nicer?"—Carol

Things to Consider

Niceness and courtesy are two different things. When we teach girls to "act nice" it's a double-edged sword. The positive side of nice (true courtesy) is rooted in mutual respect. The negative side of nice is insincere and fake. Teaching girls to act nice when they feel angry, hurt, or scared is teaching them to be emotionally dishonest and manipulative. And on top of it, that kind of niceness rarely fools others for long. We want our daughters to be thoughtful and respectful, but not at the expense of their own legitimate needs. While parents don't like to think about it, there are times girls need to be "not nice" in order to protect themselves emotionally or physically. We want to teach her to respect herself and others, and also teach her how to handle it when someone else is disrespectful of her.

What to Say and Do

1–7 YEARS OLD

Notice when you tell or praise her for "being nice." Try to use other words, and be specific in describing the behavior you're commenting on.

- I want you and Cassie to play without grabbing things from each other. You can use words and say what you want, but no grabbing.

- It was thoughtful of you to let Raisa go down the slide first. She appreciated it and let you go first the next time.

8–13 YEARS OLD

When she uses the word nice to describe someone or something, ask her to describe more specifically what she means.

- It sounds like Josh is a good friend. Tell me about him.

- The kids in the band welcomed you as a new member, and that felt good.

Teach her that she can be respectful of others without accepting mean or manipulative behavior from them.

- You're sensitive to her feelings and you want to be nice, but it sounds like she's very insensitive to yours. That's not a real friendship because it's a one-way street. You're being caring and she's not. You can take care of yourself by not hanging out with her.

- That hurt your feelings. You can tell him you didn't like it without being mean.

- You want to respect the coach, but you feel he was being abusive when he screamed at you. I'll set up a meeting so we can talk with him about it together.

14 AND UP

When she starts to have romances, she may feel a lot of pressure to always act nice—even when she's not feeling good. Encourage her to keep in touch with her authentic feelings and express them.

- I know you don't want to hurt Marty's feelings, but it's important to be honest. You can tell him you don't want to date anymore. He might feel hurt, but as long as you are kind and honest in how you say it, how he feels isn't your responsibility.

- It's hard when one person feels in love and the other person doesn't. Even though you're sad that your feelings aren't returned, it's better to know the truth than have a fake relationship.

Help her practice how to be honest and respect others at the same time.

- It sounds like you need to tell Leonie how you're feeling. Does doing that worry you? There are probably a few different ways you could say it. What's one way?

- When that man was hassling you at the bus stop you did the right thing by telling him firmly that you didn't like it and to stop it. And it was very smart to start talking with one of the other people waiting there.

Words, Phrases, and Actions to Use

- Honest

- Authentic

- Real

- True

- Respect

- Describe people and behavior with words other than "nice" or "not nice."

What Not to Say and Do

Don't teach her to be nice regardless of how she's being treated. Don't say,

- Be nice no matter how other people act.
- Be nicer and maybe they'll like you better.

Don't teach her to cover up feelings like anger, fear, or confusion by "acting nice." Don't say,

- Don't tell him how you feel—it might upset him.
- Act nice and it will work out fine.

Words and Phrases to Avoid

- Nice
- Control your feelings
- How you act is more important than how you feel.
- Don't get carried away.
- Just be nice.
- Girls should always be nice.

OVERSCHEDULING

"Sometimes during the year, it feels like my daughter and I don't have enough time to have even a simple conversation that isn't about logistics because she is so busy with activities. Well, I guess I have a lot of things scheduled, too. But then during vacation, she complains about being bored. Isn't there some middle ground?"—Judie

Things to Consider

We want our girls to succeed so they'll feel better about themselves, be well liked, get into a good college, and so on. But too often, both parents and daughters equate success exclusively with public and tangible accomplishments, like number of goals scored or solo recitals performed. But success in childhood (and beyond) also relies on discovering yourself, exercising your imagination, reflecting on life, and pure play. All of these "accomplishments" are nurtured by unstructured time and the freedom to wander everywhere from your mind to a foreign country. Therefore, we have to keep a balance in our kids' schedules and keep an especially keen eye on the temptation to value our own parental worth by how well our children perform.

What to Say and Do

1–7 YEARS OLD
Start early to encourage and reward unstructured play that isn't prescripted. Play is her role, and it's for her benefit, not anyone else's.

- I've got the whole afternoon off. Let's go for a long walk.

- That village you built with your blocks is so cool!

- Let's have a "we can only play with toys that don't have batteries" day.

8–13 YEARS OLD
Keep time and space open for unstructured, childlike play.

- Let's go see how big a leaf pile we can make, and then jump all over it.

- Anytime you want to shoot hoops, I'll rebound for you.

- What did you find today when you went exploring?

Don't rescue her from boredom. Boredom is a great motivator, if you let it do its work.

- I know you can figure out something to do; you usually come up with something very creative.

- No, I won't take you to the mall. Take the afternoon to brainstorm and dream about what you want to do this summer.

14 AND UP
Encourage open-ended time for play and reflection.

- It was so cool to see you and Ruthie being so goofy with your old hand puppets.

- I like sitting quietly with you while we read or write in our journals.

Make time and space for unorganized, natural, and spontaneous activities.

- Let's go camping this summer without all the fancy gear and just see what happens.

- There's a pickup softball game over in the park; let's go join it.

Be patient with boredom and use it to encourage creativity.

Words and Phrases to Use

- You can do it!

- I love what you create out of what you have.

- That's a great insight; I like how you make time for that kind of reflection.

What Not to Say and Do

Don't judge her worth by her performance. Don't say,

- Can't you do better than that?

- What do you mean you don't want lessons?

- If you don't even want to *try out* for the team, I have no use for you.

Don't fall for fads that undervalue the basics. Don't say,

- This battery-powered car is lots more fun than your Legos.

- You have to use the computer; you don't want to be stupid, do you?

Resources

The Over-Scheduled Child: Avoiding the Hyper-Parenting Trap by Alvin Rosenfeld and Nicole Wise. Griffin, 2001.

PARTIES AND SLEEPOVERS

"Kirsten's in fifth grade and just got invited to her first girl-boy party. I didn't expect the whole dating thing to come up so soon. She's much too young for that. But she desperately wants to go to the party. How do I decide what to do?"—Lillian

Things to Consider

Parties and sleepovers are a big part of girls' social life starting in the middle elementary years. A girl's first sleepover at a friend's house is a definite rite of passage for you both. Most girls really enjoy getting together, playing games, watching videos, and talking. The downside of all-girl parties is that they might become occasions for social bullying by cliques (excluded girls don't get invited) or for similar behavior at the parties if they're not adequately supervised. Many girls will continue to have girl-only parties throughout their teen years, and that's healthy.

Girl-boy parties are a different terrain for parents. Often they start happening before girls and boys are actually dating or having romances. This can be good, especially when they're a way for girls and boys to interact in an informal, group situation that doesn't involve pairing up. It's a chance for them to learn something about social interaction with each other with nothing at stake. It's also a chance for parents to get a sense of the group their daughter is friends with. This is all assuming that the parties are well supervised by adults. As a girl gets older, you need to negotiate firm rules about the types of parties she can and can't attend. Ultimately, in her last couple years of high school, you want to be able to trust her judgment enough that she handles her own decisions as long as she keeps you informed about where she is and honors the curfew you agree on.

What to Say and Do

8–13 YEARS OLD

Know the families whose houses she's going to and be sure you're comfortable with the situations and supervision. Give them info about how to contact you if you won't be home. If she has special needs or concerns about a sleepover, ask if the host family is comfortable with that.

- Elly invited you to sleep over. That sounds fun. I'll call her dad to find out the details.

- I told the Shapiros about your insulin testing, and when we drop you off, I'll show them how to help you with it.

Have clear guidelines for her about party situations that are green light, yellow light, and red light. Be specific about what each type is so she can learn to assess them herself.

- We've come up with guidelines about what kind of parties you can definitely go to or definitely not go to. The "yellow lights" are ones we need to look at case by case.

- A "red light" is if there are no adults in the house, there are high school kids there, or kids are drinking, smoking, using drugs, or making out.

Welcome her friends to your house at any time. You can get to know them and they can get to know you. It's a good indication that your daughter is comfortable with her friends when she brings them home.

14 AND UP

Continue with clear rules that recognize she's more mature, and put additional trust in her judgment. Make an agreement that you will come pick her up anywhere if she calls you and you won't ask questions about it until the next day. If she shows a lapse in judgment, have a clear, reasonable consequence agreed upon ahead of time.

- It's still nonnegotiable that there has to be an adult in the house and no drinking, smoking, drugs, or sex going on.

- You need to call us when you leave one place and go to another. You need to be home by midnight.

If she does things you don't want her to, tell her openly and calmly about the concerns or fears you have about it. And use the consequence you already told her about.

- I was very worried when you weren't home by curfew and didn't call me. You knew you were safe, but I didn't.

If you did things as a teenager that you regret, this is the age when it's appropriate to tell her about your experience and the consequences and why you wish you hadn't done it. Give her the facts and your feelings, but don't make it sound worse than it was.

Words and Phrases to Use

- Fun
- Communication
- Keeping in touch
- Rules

- Maturity
- Curfew
- I trust you.
- You have good judgment in friends.

What Not to Say and Do

Don't prohibit her from going to all parties. Don't say,

- I know what kind of stupid stuff goes on at parties in junior high.

- No way you're going.

Don't distrust her or her friends unless they give you clear cause to do that. Don't say,

- If boys are there, they'll just want to get you drunk.

- You can't bring those kids in our house. They'll make a mess.

Resources

"Trust Me, Mom—Everyone Else Is Going!" The New Rules for Mothering Adolescent Girls by Roni Cohen-Sandler. Penguin, 2003.

PEER PRESSURE

"I'm worried that Liz is hanging out with a group that's kind of 'fast' about drinking and sex. I don't think she really wants to do those things, but these kids are in the neighborhood and have been her friends since fifth grade. I'm not sure she can resist the peer pressure to do some things she wouldn't do otherwise. Should I just tell her she can't go out with them anymore?"—Bernie

Things to Consider

Peer pressure can definitely encourage your daughter to do things she wouldn't do otherwise—both negative and positive. It *does* matter who her friends are and what their values, activities, and ambitions are. Most people tend to act like the people they spend a lot of time with. If you're concerned about what her friends are interested in, it's important to talk with your daughter about that in a calm, open, nonaccusatory way.

What *doesn't* help is making snap judgments or basing your opinion of her friends on how they dress or their family's status. Those things are superficial, and your criticism might make her feel she has to defend them, even when she doesn't agree with them. But if you know or suspect that her friends are doing dangerous or illegal things, you're wise to put firm limits on when and how she spends time with those friends (mainly with adult supervision). She's still maturing, and her good judgment may be diluted by wanting to fit in with her peers. Don't blame her for that feeling, but guide her away from the unhealthy behaviors.

What to Say and Do

1–7 YEARS OLD

Encourage her to follow her own mind and not just do something because other kids are doing it.

- You have a strong mind and do what you think is right. I like that.

- You really know what you want and that's great.

8–13 YEARS OLD

If she starts to find different values and goals between her and her friends, just listen and ask gentle questions when she talks about it.

- It sounds like things are changing between you and Julie. That sounds difficult.

- You sound worried about Becka's new friends. You still want to be loyal to Becka, but you don't like some of the things she does with that other crowd.

- How do you feel about it?

If she starts showing behavior that concerns you, talk with her about her behavior/responsibility, and don't blame it on her friends.

Create adult-supervised situations for her to be with peers you may be concerned about.

14 AND UP

If you're concerned about how her friends act, convey your concern for them and their well-being.

- It seems like Tricia has really changed a lot in the past few months. I get the feeling she might be having sex. I'm concerned about her protecting herself with birth control and STD prevention.

- In tenth grade my oldest friend started drinking a lot and we grew apart. I was really confused and didn't know what to do. Now I realize I might have helped her by talking with a professional about it.

Words and Phrases to Use

- Behavior
- Your values
- Choices
- Options
- Caring

- Concern
- Safety
- Loyalty
- Good friend
- How do you feel when they do that?

What Not to Say and Do

Don't try to turn her against her friends. Don't say,

- Those kids are losers. Why do you hang out with them?
- You have to choose between them and us.

Don't fault her for being affected by peer pressure. Don't say,

- You're just weak and can't say no to them.
- You have no guts.
- Don't you have a mind of your own?

Words and Phrases to Avoid

- Forbid
- Never
- Bad news

- No future
- Jailbait
- No contact at all

Resources

Girls: What's So Bad about Being Good? How to Have Fun, Survive the Preteen Years, and Remain True to Yourself by Harriet S. Mosatche and Liz Lawner. Crown Publishing, 2001.

The Second Family: Dealing with Peer Power, Pop Culture, the Wall of Silence—and Other Challenges of Raising Today's Teens by Ron Taffel. St. Martin's Press, 2002.

PERFECTIONISM

"Nula is beautiful and smart and talented in so many ways. I'm very proud of her. But she can find something wrong with everything, and so she doesn't seem to get much satisfaction from all the things she does well. In her eyes there's always something lacking. How can I make her less judgmental of herself?"—Ibrahim

Things to Consider

High standards and expectations can help our daughters to do their best. But perfectionism is unattainable and an unhealthy extreme. It keeps her chronically dissatisfied and can also stop her from trying things. It can be a primary cause of procrastination and underachievement. It's important for parents to distinguish between a girl's appropriate self-criticism (which will help her improve) and unrealistic perfectionism. Healthy criticism focuses on specific actions and habits—things she can reasonably improve. She can learn to analyze and critique those things without feeling like there's something wrong with her central self. While perfectionism may seem similar, it focuses instead on things like her basic personality, physical and intellectual abilities, and other things that are out of any person's control. Perfectionism leaves her feeling helpless and inadequate.

What to Say and Do

1–7 YEARS OLD

If she shows signs of perfectionism at this age, give her consistent help with recognizing and reducing its effects on her.

- You feel frustrated that your painting didn't turn out the way you wanted. It's a beautiful painting to me because of the colors and shapes you chose and it reminds me of you. I'm going to hang it by my desk.

Provide her with a reliable daily structure without making it rigid.

Help her cope with both predictable and unexpected changes.

- You like to have your special granola for breakfast, but at Poppa's house he doesn't have that. I know that's hard for you. Let's think now about what you can have instead like some of his cereal or eggs and toast.

- We didn't expect it to rain today so you didn't wear your boots. We can dry everything off and it'll be fine.

8–13 YEARS OLD

If she hasn't been perfectionistic but starts showing signs, it's probably a way of coping with stress and trying to gain some control. Get at the underlying cause.

- I've noticed you're being kind of hard on yourself lately. What's going on with that?

Admit your own perfectionism, work on it openly, and make it a game to catch each other at it.

- There I go, expecting to be Little Ms. Perfect again! How silly of me.

- I didn't realize I was doing it—thanks for telling me.

14 AND UP
Emphasize that creativity and energy give more satisfaction than perfectionism.

- It all looked perfect but it seemed kind of cold and lifeless—not as interesting or fun.

- Your passion shines out in your playing the most when you're not trying to do it perfectly.

Words, Phrases, and Actions to Use

- Excellence is not perfection.

- Perfection is unreal.

- Perfectionism sucks the enjoyment out of things.

- Why do you think you want it to be perfect?

What Not to Say and Do

Don't let perfectionism limit her experiences. Don't say,

- Since you're not the best player it's OK to quit.

- If you can't do it right, it's better not to do it at all.

- If you tried harder you could get it perfect.

Words and Phrases to Avoid

- That's perfect!

- You're just not talented.

- You don't care enough to do it right.

- There's only one right way and that's not it.

Resources

Freeing Our Families from Perfectionism by Thomas S. Greenspon. Free Spirit Publishing, 2001.

PERSONALITY

"My daughter Natalie is quiet and thoughtful with a lot of depth. She gets overlooked in groups because she's not demanding attention or acting out. I know what a special person she is, but wonder if I need to teach her how to be more extroverted so other people appreciate her."—Mala

Things to Consider

Scientists believe that personality traits like extroversion and introversion are basically determined at birth. What's most important is to help our daughters understand their personalities and value their traits, especially if those traits (like introversion) are less common and less appreciated in our culture.

The Myers-Briggs personality types are very helpful in understanding the strengths and weaknesses each of us has. Understanding them and teaching your daughter about them can help her feel comfortable and value her own strengths. It will also help her understand and communicate effectively with other personality types.

When she knows herself, she's better prepared for difficult or stressful situations. She has a strong foundation for friendship and teamwork. Knowing and valuing herself will also help her accept others and the ways they are different, which makes for better relationships, even within the family. It can be a powerful tool for reducing conflict when we feel we understand and accept each other, no matter how different we are.

What to Say and Do

1–7 YEARS OLD

Make occasional nonjudgmental observations about the personalities in your family.

- I really like to have things organized when I sit down at my desk. But Dad doesn't care about that. We're totally different that way.

- After you play with friends, you like to spend some quiet time by yourself. On the other hand, your brother likes to be with other people nearly all the time. It's good that you both know what you need.

Read books about the Myers-Briggs personality types and think about your own type and how it interacts with your daughter's type.

8 AND UP

Introduce her to concepts of personality types, using a book intended to give a basic understanding. Emphasize this is just one aspect of understanding herself and other people.

Help her feel good about her personality traits by focusing on the benefits more than the drawbacks.

- Introverts are people with very deep feelings inside. I can see your deep feelings come out in your creativity in art.

- Intuitive people see the big picture and imagine a lot of new things the way you do.

Help her learn to cope proactively with the weaknesses of her traits by developing strategies and sharing your own techniques.

- People like you and me tend to have a hard time making decisions because we don't want to close off any possibilities. It helps me to narrow it down to two choices and then pick one. If there are too many options, I have a very hard time. And it helps to remember I can always change my mind later if I want to.

Help her use personality types to understand her frustration with people who have different traits from hers.

- I can see it bugs you when you're telling me about your feelings and all I want to do is come up with a logical solution. I'm trying to stop doing that. You can remind me that you just want to talk and don't want a solution.

- You and Millie are great friends even though you have very different personalities. You balance each other out really well with your opposite strengths, but I know it can be hard to understand why she does things sometimes.

- Our family is kind of like your hockey team. If we all had the same personalities, we'd be a weaker team, just like if everyone on your hockey team was a great goalie but no one was good at scoring.

Words and Phrases to Use

- Understand
- Many ways for people to be
- Self-awareness
- Know yourself

- Acceptance
- Balance
- Teamwork

What Not to Say and Do

Don't be judgmental about her personality and criticize things she can't change. Don't say,

- If you were more outgoing, you'd have more friends. You don't even try.

- It's so easy to be realistic, but your head is always in the clouds. Stop it!

Don't compare personality traits in a competitive way. Don't say,

- I wish you were neat and organized like your sister.

- It's better to be logical and not concerned with how people feel.

Words and Phrases to Avoid

- Why are you like that?

- What's the matter with you?

- That's a stupid way to be.

- If only you would change . . .

Resources

Gifts Differing: Understanding Personality Type by Isabel Briggs-Myers. Consulting Psychologists Press, 1995.

The Highly Sensitive Person: How to Thrive When the World Overwhelms You by Elaine N. Aron. Bantam Doubleday Dell, 1997.

The Introvert Advantage: How to Thrive in an Extrovert World by Marti Olsen. Workman Publishing, 2002.

Please Understand Me II: Temperament, Character, Intelligence by David Keirsey. Prometheus Nemesis, 1998.

What Type Am I? Discover Who You Really Are by Renee Baron. Penguin, 1998.

PIERCINGS AND TATTOOS

"I don't have any problem with piercings since they'll close up if not kept open. But a tattoo is such a permanent thing. I don't want Erin to get tattoos."—Terri

Things to Consider

Parents have widely varying levels of concern about daughters getting piercings and tattoos. Some are fine with anything as long as it's done in a safe, sanitary situation. Others are opposed to all of it. Most parents fall somewhere in the middle.

Your daughter is likely to feel that piercings and tattoos are no big deal. She might feel that it's a way to celebrate her body and decorate it, similar to how you may feel about jewelry. It might also be part of her identifying with a peer group. Your feelings will probably evolve as she gets older, and you may be fine with her doing something at sixteen that you prohibited earlier. It's not wise to make this a major battleground with mid to older teens unless you feel her health is in danger. There are more important concerns to save your battles for at this point.

What to Say and Do

1–7 YEARS OLD
She might want ear piercing to feel more grown up. You can let her do it now or defer the decision until she's older.

- We'll talk about that when you're nine.
- You need to be older to take care of pierced ears.

8–13 YEARS OLD
Most of her peers will get pierced ears at this age. Be sure she knows how to keep them clean and infection free.

- Whenever they feel sore or look red, you need to clean them with alcohol in the morning and at night.

If you don't want her to get any piercings, explain why. Allow her to explain why she wants to.

- Our religious beliefs don't allow for ear piercing.
- I want you to be an adult before you make that kind of decision.

14 AND UP
If she wants to get tattoos or tongue or other piercings you feel uncomfortable about, tell her why.

- Tattoos are really permanent. Even if they're removed with lasers, there's still scarring.
- I think it can be unsafe with the needles that are used. How would you be sure it's totally antiseptic?
- I feel like it's a sign of sexual availability, and I'm not comfortable with that.

Tell her when you'll let her make these decisions on her own.

- Once you're sixteen, you can make that decision on your own, and I won't bug you about it.

- I feel so strongly against tattoos that you'll need to wait until you're not living at home to do that if you still want to.

Words and Phrases to Use

- Clean

- Sanitary

- Maturity

- My values

What Not to Say and Do

Don't refuse to listen to her feelings or discuss it. Don't say,

- I told you no. Don't bring it up ever again!

- I'll never let you do that.

Don't insult people who have tattoos or piercings. Don't say,

- Only slutty women have tattoos.

- That's disgusting.

Words and Phrases to Avoid

- Gross

- Filthy

- Indecent

- Barbaric
- Primitive

Resources

Tattooing and Body Piercing: Understanding the Risks by Kathleen Winkler. Enslow Publishers, 2002.

POPULARITY

"Nadia's 'best' friends dumped her because we bought the wrong kind of jeans (according to Nadia). Now she's depressed about not being in the popular group and feels like a misfit. I want her to know that kind of popularity is short lived and not worth coveting, but she thinks I'm just out of touch and don't understand what she's going through."—Gayle

Things to Consider

Popularity creates a social hierarchy that is characteristic of most human groups. And if we parents are honest, we'll admit that we *still* feel that way in some situations. We can relate to the pressures our daughters feel. But relating to them doesn't mean we want to buy into the pressure to be popular if we feel it's harmful for them.

At the same time, remember that popularity itself isn't evil. In some schools or groups, popularity can mean behaviors that you support, like community involvement or good grades or good sportswomanship. On the harmful side, popularity can be a way of excluding or ostracizing certain people or groups for petty or biased reasons. The key is to teach her to distinguish the behaviors associated with popularity in a particular group and support her making decisions about the group based on her values.

What to Say and Do

8–13 YEARS OLD

These can be the most intense years for wanting popularity. Help her understand the dynamics and fleeting nature of popularity and her lack of control over it.

- Popularity can be like clothes that are in one year and out the next. It doesn't usually last.

- What really matters is being true to your own beliefs, whether they are popular or not. That can be tough to do sometimes.

- Since popularity is decided by other people, not you, you can't control it. That's hard to accept.

An overwhelming need to be popular can indicate insecurity that you want to help her resolve.

- It seems that you feel more confident when you feel part of the popular group. Do you have thoughts about why?

14 AND UP

Popularity pressure may continue even though she and her peers are a bit more mature. Keep an open ear for the pains and frustrations of her wanting to feel part of a group.

- Feeling part of a group is very important to you right now. I understand.

Help her problem solve about finding groups she feels good being part of.

- Some people on the debate team have become such good friends for you.

- There's only one "popular" group and lots and lots of other groups. Some of the other groups might be where you fit.

Words and Phrases to Use

- How do you feel inside about this group?

- Does the popular group do the things you care about?

- Popularity changes often.

- Can you be yourself with them?

- What do they value?

- What is their popularity based on?

What Not to Say and Do

Don't dismiss the whole issue and her feelings about it as irrelevant. Don't say,

- Popularity is totally unimportant. We don't need to talk about it.

- That's so childish; you're more mature than that.

Words and Phrases to Avoid

- Just ignore the whole thing.

- I don't want to hear any more about it.

- That's just immature girl stuff.

- Get over it!

- You know what's popular, so just do that.

Resources

Mom, They're Teasing Me: Helping Your Child Solve Social Problems by Michael Thompson. Ballantine Books, 2002.

Odd Girl Speaks Out: Girls Write about Bullies, Cliques, Popularity, and Jealousy by Rachel Simmons. Harcourt, 2004.

Why Doesn't Anybody Like Me? A Guide to Raising Socially Confident Kids by Hara Estroff Marano. HarperCollins, 1998.

PORNOGRAPHY

"I feel overwhelmed by the number of ads and other things that use sex, sex, sex to sell things and make them attractive. Listen, I'm trying hard to help my daughter celebrate her emerging sexuality because I think sexuality is central to who we are. But it seems like the media is getting more and more perverse and pornographic in its imagery. That completely undermines what I'm trying to teach her, and I don't know what to do."—Bruno

Things to Consider

Media and marketing are using more pornographic imagery and manipulating healthy sexuality into crass titillation to sell products. In addition, there's a steady increase in the number and variety of purely pornographic magazines, TV shows, and Web sites.

The challenge of parents is threefold. One, we must not put our heads in the sand and pretend that these images and messages aren't visible to and affecting our daughters. Two, we must clearly tell our kids that perverse use of sexuality is wrong and openly challenge those who pervert it for profit. Third, we must "walk the talk" in our own lives, especially dads. As fathering author Joe Kelly puts it, "A man who tells his daughter that she can be anything she wants to be, then turns around and picks up a copy of *Playboy,* may as well have saved his damn breath. His actions tell her that it's OK to objectify women, reinforcing a stubborn cultural barrier for his daughter."

What to Say and Do

8–13 YEARS OLD

Your use of porn will influence your children, even if you think you're "hiding" it from them. Others' use of porn also affects them, so confront it openly.

- You are important for who you are, not for what anyone thinks about your body.

- I'm tired of seeing so many commercials and stores using women's bodies to sell stuff. Want to write a protest letter with me to an advertiser?

- I just found out that our long-distance company owns a ton of porn Web sites. I'm changing companies and writing to tell them why. I think my letter would be even more powerful if you wrote it with me.

14 AND UP

Put your daughter's face in the picture. As she emerges into a sexual being, you want her valued and celebrated for all her qualities, not for what false sexualized pose she can strike.

- Sexuality is not about how much skin you can show. It is about making a connection with yourself and others spiritually, emotionally, and physically.

- Boys are interested in more than sex. They also want friendship, companionship, and connection. That was true when I was a teenager, and it's true now. (This is especially important for dads and stepdads to say to daughters *and* sons.)

- Many women who work in the porn industry were abused as girls. Most porn profits go to male-run corporations.

Actions to Use

- Recognize how often and how shamelessly "mainstream" companies use pornographic images in marketing.

- Join organizations like Dads and Daughters (www.dadsanddaughters.org) that fight back against pornography and objectification of women and girls.

What Not to Say and Do

Don't dismiss the power and symbolism of widespread pornographic imagery. Don't say,

- Boys will be boys; it's no big deal.

- Who does a little "T & A" in private hurt?

- If a woman wants to make money doing porn, no harm done.

Actions to Avoid

- Don't buy pornography.

- Refuse to remain silent about (and thus acquiesce to) pornographic imagery in "mainstream" media.

Resources

Dads and Daughters: How to Inspire, Support, and Understand Your Daughter by Joe Kelly. Broadway Books, 2003.

Men Confront Pornography, edited by Michael Kimmel. Crown Publishing, 1990.

POWER

"I want Charity to feel good about herself, but the word 'power' bothers me a little. It makes me think of manipulative, selfish people, especially women."
—Kay

Things to Consider

Power can get a bad rap. We've all heard the phrases: "power corrupts," "power hungry," and "power crazed." We wouldn't want our daughters associated with any of these aspects of power. Of course, we don't want them to be helpless victims, either. It helps to remember that power itself is neither good nor bad. It's the way people use it that's good or bad. And as far as girls are concerned, the more powerful they feel, the better.

The fact is our culture has conflicting feelings about powerful women and girls. They are often portrayed in very negative ways and labeled unnatural, threatening, or unfeminine. At the same time, girls and women are expected to be self-sufficient and independent. Girls pick up on these mixed messages and may decide to steer clear of power because it seems controversial or confusing. We can help them see power as an inner strength to have and use well to help themselves and others. Dads can play a special role in showing that they admire powerful women who work for good.

What to Say and Do

1–7 YEARS OLD
Tell her she's powerful, both physically and in other ways.

- Wow, your brain is powerful. It figured that out!

- You have the power to make people laugh at your jokes.

Provide experiences where she can feel powerful and in control of herself.

- You did that all by yourself.

8–13 YEARS OLD
Talk about power as a positive thing.

Help her be aware of the power she has to make choices and decisions.

- That's up to you; it's in your power.

- Looking at the positive side of things gives you power.

- You have the power to make the class better or worse.

Help her experience the power of being part of a group working together.

- It's so powerful the way you and your friends wrote and acted out that play.

- When your group brought the petition to the mayor, it was powerful. She really listened.

14 AND UP
Emphasize that power starts inside each person and isn't always visible in the present.

- Sometimes the power of a belief or idea isn't recognized for a long time.

- Our inner power is what gets us through the tough times.

Communicate that power includes responsibilities.

- Your friends look up to you, and that gives you both power and responsibility.

Give her opportunities to interact with powerful women as much as possible.

Talk about positive and negative uses of power and how they're different.

Words and Phrases to Use

- Power for good
- Inner power
- Power of faith
- Strong beliefs
- Strength

- Energy
- Accomplishment
- Power of caring

What Not to Say and Do

Don't tell her power is bad. Don't say,

- Everyone with power is a jerk.
- I hate those power-hungry politicians.

Don't tell her she's too powerful. Don't say,

- You're getting too big for your britches, young lady.
- People don't like powerful girls.

Words and Phrases to Avoid

- Bossy

- Demanding

- Power is evil.

- Power corrupts.

- Boys like girls who need to be taken care of.

- Powerful women intimidate men.

- If you're too powerful, no one will marry you.

Resources

Girl Thoughts: A Girl's Own Incredible, Powerful and Absolutely Private Journal by Judith Harlan. Walker & Co., 2000.

PREGNANCY AND PARENTING

"The statistics about teenagers getting pregnant terrify me. I don't want Maria to get negative feelings about sex like I did, but I don't want her to get pregnant until she's old enough to be a good parent. How do I communicate both things to her?"—Sylvia

Things to Consider

Teen pregnancy declined in the 1990s, but the US rate is still higher than in any other developed nation. Pregnancy comes as a shock to some teens and is sought by others. In many situations, girls will deal with all the momentous decisions of pregnancy on their own—whether to have an abortion, give the baby up for adoption, or take on the responsibility herself. Parenthood is a very heavy responsibility for a teenager. It's not the end of the world, but it is a very tough road to take. We want to support her in such a difficult time, but we don't want to take over her responsibility for her.

Some teen mothers say having a baby is what gave them motivation they'd been lacking to get more education and work for a better future for themselves. As parents, we'd rather our daughters find another way to increased motivation. We want them to be able to finish their own maturing before they're responsible for another life, we want our potential grandchildren to get mature parenting, and we certainly know the demands and the rewards included in being parents. So the question most of us ask is, How do we help a girl not get pregnant before she's ready to make a mature, conscious decision?

A study in the April 2002 issue of *Pediatrics* showed self-esteem plays an apparent role in the loss of virginity among adolescents. Self-esteem had opposite effects on young girls and young boys. Young girls with high self-esteem were less likely to engage in early sexual activity, while boys with high self-esteem were more likely.

Ultimately, you want to find a way to honor your values and also safeguard your daughter's future. Start by informing yourself of the realities of teen pregnancy rates and the scientific research that's been done on what is successful in prevention. For her well-being, set aside any prejudices you may have about certain sources of information and look at a variety of material and advice. That way you'll know what research says and also have a choice of approaches to take. Take your daughter's personality and behavior into account as you decide how to approach this with her. And start early, giving her clear facts as well as statements about your values.

What to Say and Do

8–13 YEARS OLD

Talk in daily life about what it's like to be a parent. Be open about all the responsibilities it includes. Talk about the rewards and also the sacrifices or struggles of parenthood matter-of-factly. Talk about pregnancy as a decision she has control over, not just an accident that happens. Regularly give her factual and specific age-appropriate information about how pregnancy occurs and can be prevented. Present this information separately from talking about your values. If you're uncomfortable doing this, get her qualified adult help (doctor, counselor, clinic) to do it.

- You can prevent pregnancy two ways: by not having sex and by correctly using certain kinds of birth control.

- Here is how you track your menstrual cycle.

Share your values about teen sex, abortion, and pregnancy. Talk honestly about your experiences as a teen and your pregnancies, teen or later.

- Dad and I were using unreliable birth control when you were conceived. We didn't plan to have a baby yet.

- Of course I love you very much, but I wish we had waited a few years to start our family. We would have been more prepared.

- I would like you to be an adult before you make a decision as big as having a baby.

- I feel that when I started having sex, I wasn't ready. I did it to please my boyfriend. But it turned out that I felt guilty about it until I was older.

Ahead of time, think through how you will respond if you find out she's having sex or is pregnant. Discuss it with her other parent and stepparents.

14 AND UP

Understand that the likelihood of her having sex before the end of high school is high. Be informed, not naïve. Talk with her about the statistics, peer pressure, and so forth.

Accept that ultimately when to have sex is a decision she will make for herself. Listen carefully and respectfully to what she tells you about her values.

- In the end, it's up to you to make that decision. I want you to feel prepared and be able to think it through.

- The desire for sex can be very strong and that's a good thing. My hope is that you'll be able to balance that with doing what you decide is best for you. I wasn't able to do that until I was eighteen. Before that I was just looking for approval.

Continue to let her know and see your values.

- I feel very strongly that it's important to know someone very well and to feel deeply committed before you think about having sex.

- We believe in waiting until you're married to have sex. I know it's unusual, but Mom and I did that and we're glad.

- We want you to know you can always talk to us about this, and we'll listen to you with an open mind, no matter what.

Words and Phrases to Use

- Responsibility
- Trust
- Maturity

- Birth control
- Abstinence
- Sexual desire is natural.

What Not to Say and Do

Don't hide the difficulties or overromanticize babies and parenthood. Don't say things like

- Babies make you happy, no matter what.
- Babies are easy; they sleep most of the time.

Don't fail to give her a lot of facts and information. Don't say,

- You can find out about that when you get married.
- You're too young to ask about that.
- All you need to know is don't have sex and you won't get pregnant.

Words and Phrases to Avoid

- You shouldn't even think about that.
- You have to tell boys no.
- Boys can't control themselves, so you have to.
- It's your fault.

Resources

Kids Still Having Kids: Talking about Teen Pregnancy by Janet Bode. Scholastic, 1999.

Teen Pregnancy by Jennifer A. Hurley. Gale Group, 2000.

Teen Pregnancy by Mary Nolan. Heinemann, 2002.

Your Baby's First Year: A Guide for Teenage Parents by Jeanne Warren Lindsay. Morning Glory Press, 2004.

Your Pregnancy and Newborn Journey: A Guide for Pregnant Teens by Jeanne Warren Lindsay, Jean Brunelli and P. H. Brunelli. Morning Glory Press, 2004.

PREJUDICE

"I volunteer at my daughter's middle school, and I've always thought of it as a fairly healthy place for students. But I recently took a workshop on identifying and reducing racism in myself and the world around me. Ever since then, the school looks a lot worse to me. It seems stuck in a cruel system of stereotypes and judging people by their appearance—and not just skin color. Nothing I do seems to help."—Susan

Things to Consider

Prejudice—racism, sexism, or other discrimination—is built so systemically in so many of our environments that it's often hard for us to acknowledge, let alone combat. Being the victim of prejudice can leave a girl feeling devastated and helpless. Others may demean her for her skin color, size, gender, ethnicity, ability/disability (even something as common as wearing glasses), sexuality, socioeconomic class, religion, family members, neighborhood, or other qualities. We must help her resist bigotry's impact on her life and fight the systems that reinforce racism, sexism, homophobia, "lookism," ageism, and other biases. Most important, we must not tolerate bigotry in ourselves or our children.

What to Say and Do

1–7 YEARS OLD

Intervene immediately when you see or hear bigotry anywhere in her presence, no matter what the source: her, you, a family member, playmate, or others.

- It is wrong to judge people by how they look. What's most important about you is who you are inside. The same is true for every other person on earth.

- It is wrong to say that, and let me explain why.

- Mom, that is a bigoted statement, and I do not want you expressing opinions like that around us.

8 AND UP

Expose her to a diversity of people and experiences. When she sees prejudice help her respond constructively whether she is a victim or a bystander.

- Why do you think the group is excluding Jocelyn?

- What do you think would work to do or say in that situation?

Help her reject bigotry when it is directed at her by feeling proud of her race, gender, ethnicity, and so on. Help her find a supportive group of friends.

- Let me tell you stories about the relatives Grandma has in her photo album.

- We don't let people like that define us. We give up our power if we do.

Help her identify contradictions and harmful stereotypes.

- What do you know about Lilith's religion?

- Do you think blondes enjoy life more than brunettes?

- What do you actually know about what Mary Beth can do, even though she's in a wheelchair?

Actions to Use

■ Keep your children's bookcase stocked with stories featuring strong characters from a wide range of backgrounds and heritages.

■ If your daughter is being harmed by a scenario she can't handle alone, step in. Demand that other adults and institutions join you in creating a solution.

■ Ask your child's principal to order the FREE twice-yearly magazine, *Teaching Tolerance,* for every teacher and staff member in the school.

■ Draw on your family history to build her self-worth.

■ Draw on cultural and women's history to build her self-worth.

■ Support her when she's a target of bias; acknowledge her experience.

■ Learn and talk about groups of people different from you, and display diversity in your home and workplace.

■ Be open and honest about differences between people. We're not all the same, and that's something to cherish.

■ Model acceptance and tolerance.

What Not to Say and Do

Don't let her or your prejudicial attitudes or beliefs go unchallenged. Don't say,

■ What can you expect from black people?

■ Stay away from those faggots.

■ Boys can't do that. They're boys!

■ You can't do that. You're a girl!

■ That kid must be retarded; he looks so goofy.

Don't minimize her when she experiences intolerance. Don't say,

- They were only joking. It's no big deal.

- What do you expect from people like that? Forget about it.

Resources

Don't Laugh at Me by Steve Seskin. Ten Speed Press, 2002.

Everyday Acts against Racism: Raising Children in a Multiracial World, edited by Maureen T. Reddy. Seal Press, 1996.

40 Ways to Raise a Nonracist Child by Barbara Mathais. HarperPerennial, 1996.

The Freedom Writers Diary: How a Group of Teens Used the Power of the Pen to Wage a War Against Intolerance by Erin Gruwell and the Freedom Writers. Broadway Books, 1999.

Hate Hurts: How Children Learn and Unlearn Prejudice by Caryl Stern-LaRosa and Ellen Hofheimer Bettmann. Chicken House, 2000.

My Sisters' Voices: Teenage Girls of Color Speak Out by Iris Jacob. Henry Holt, 2002.

Raising Black Children: Two Leading Psychiatrists Confront the Educational, Social, and Emotional Problems Facing Black Children by James P. Comer, MD, and Alvin F. Poussaint, MD. Plume, 1992.

Teaching Tolerance: Raising Open-Minded, Empathetic Children by Sara Bullard. Main Street Books, 1997.

Teaching Tolerance magazine: www.tolerance.org/teach/expand/mag/index.jsp

Uprooting Racism: How White People Can Work for Racial Justice by Paul Kivel. New Society, 1995.

Gay, Lesbian and Straight Education Network: www.glsen.org

Operation Respect: www.dontlaugh.org

Tolerance.org: www.tolerance.org (resources and news for parents, teachers and kids).

PRIVACY AND SECRETS

"Malika used to tell me everything. But now she's a closed book and I wonder why. I ask her questions and she gives me monosyllabic answers. Could she be hiding something I need to know about?"—Aimee

Things to Consider

Girls and moms are often very close until girls reach their preteens. Sometimes you might even wish for a little *less* togetherness. But all of a sudden your talkative child seems totally uncommunicative with you. At the same time, she spends hours phoning and e-mailing friends, so you know she hasn't forgotten how to talk! This change might happen gradually or it could be sudden, which makes it even harder to understand.

Her need to be more private and keep secrets from her parents as she gets older is normal. She's growing up and starting to rely on people outside the family as her support system. There will probably be times when she clearly doesn't want to talk with you or want you to pry into her life. So how do you know she's not getting secretive because of drug abuse or depression or other harmful behaviors she wants to hide from you? Is it OK to straighten up her room occasionally so you can see what's in her drawers and closet? The key is to start building trust with your daughter.

What to Say and Do

1–7 YEARS OLD

Help her learn the difference between secrets she can keep and secrets she needs to tell for safety or support.

- When someone tells you a secret that upsets you, you can talk to me about it. That's not breaking your promise.

- Keeping a friend's secret is loyal as long as no one could be hurt by it.

Teach her that every person deserves privacy. It's a sign of respect.

- When your older brother is in the bathroom with the door shut, you have to knock and wait for him to say it's OK before you go in.

8–13 YEARS OLD

Respect her growing desire for privacy; it's part of her gradually making her own life.

- Your journal is private, and I would never read it without talking with you first.

- If the door is closed, I'll knock and wait for you to answer.

If you have a concern about increased secrecy, talk directly with her about it.

- You're spending a lot of time in your room with the door closed, and I wonder about it.

- I smelled marijuana smoke coming from your room.

- There seemed to be more phone calls than usual tonight between you and Debbie. I'm curious.

14 AND UP

Respect the privacy boundaries she sets; this shows you understand she's growing up. At the same time, show her you will always listen (and suspend judgment while she's talking) when she wants to talk.

- If you'd like to talk about it, I'll listen and not say anything right away.

Respond supportively and warmly when she comes to you and wants to talk, even if it's not the most convenient time.

- I really want to hear what you have to say. It's very late and I'm sleepy, but I'll stay awake as long as I can.

Keep the confidences she shares with you. If she tells you secrets of her friends and you feel you must tell someone else, explain why to her before you do it.

Share your life and thoughts and feelings with her, appropriate to her level of maturity.

Words and Phrases to Use

- Loyalty
- Good secrets, bad secrets
- Respect privacy
- Trust

- Support
- Listen
- Your own life

What Not to Say and Do

Don't invade her privacy by snooping in her room, e-mail, or journal. Don't say,

- As long as you live in this house, you don't have privacy.
- Kids don't have a right to privacy.
- I'm your mother; I know better than you do.
- Why don't you ever tell me anything anymore?

Actions to Avoid

- Don't try to force her to talk with you as much as she used to.

- Don't avoid talking about your concerns.

- Don't make excuses.

Resources

What Are You Doing in There? Balancing Your Need to Know with Your Adolescent's Need to Grow by Charlene Gianetti and Margaret Sagarese. Broadway Books, 2003.

PRIVILEGE

"Sometimes I don't think my daughter is aware of how good she has it com-pared to many other people around here, and around the world."—Samuel

Things to Consider

Just like us, our children have a variety of privileges that give them advantages over oth-ers. Some of these privileges are earned by us individually, and others are unearned—given to us by the structure of our culture. We want our children to be aware of and grateful for that reality.

It's also important for our daughters to be aware of unearned privileges—privileges that many of us avoid seeing. In a fascinating essay called *White Privilege: Unpacking the Invisible Knapsack,* Wellesley College's Dr. Peggy McIntosh lists advantages she has as a white person, but did not gain by her own efforts. These include "I do not have to educate my children to be aware of systemic racism for their own daily physical protection. My chief worries about them do not concern others' attitudes toward their race. I can easily buy posters, postcards, picture books, greeting cards, dolls, toys, and children's magazines featuring people of my race. I am never asked to speak for all the people of my racial group."

What to Say and Do

1–7 YEARS OLD

Help your daughter understand how privileged she is to live the way she does. Try concrete exercises that will help her learn this.

- When we say grace before dinner tonight, let's include prayers for those who are hungry today.

- We all have stuff that we don't use anymore. How about trying this for our birthdays: for every gift we receive, we will give one other possession to the shelter.

- I'll match whatever percentage of your allowance that you donate to charity.

8 AND UP

Encourage responsibility and gratitude about the advantages she has and that your family has.

- I really appreciate the way you stay on all of us about recycling as much as we can.

- I got us matching journals so we can write down five things we're grateful for at the end of every day.

- How can we stop wasting some of the things we have and get them into the hands of people who need them?

Talk about systemic unearned privilege and what you can do to eliminate racism, sexism, homophobia, and the like.

- Why do you think you were treated differently from Rosalita? What can we do about that if it happens again?

- Can you list some advantages you have that you didn't do anything to earn? What do you think about that list?

- I think you and I should each volunteer at least two hours a week at a nonprofit here in town. Which one do you think needs us the most?

Words and Phrases to Use

- What are you grateful for today?

- What can we do today to help someone who is less privileged than we are?

- What is your vision of a fair world?

- What can you sacrifice for the good of others?

What Not to Say and Do

Don't be blind to your privilege and advantages. Don't say,

- Those people wouldn't be poor if they weren't so stupid and lazy.

- It's our right to have all this stuff, and I don't care what anyone else thinks.

- If someone else gets dissed for who they are, it's not your problem.

- People who say they're discriminated against are just whining and looking for special treatment.

Words and Phrases to Avoid

- Racism isn't our problem; we're white.

- Sexism and racism aren't problems anymore. That got fixed years ago.

Resources

White Privilege: Unpacking the Invisible Knapsack by Peggy McIntosh, Wellesley Centers for Research on Women: http://seamonkey.ed.asu.edu/~mcisaac/emc598ge/Unpacking.html

PUBERTY AND PERIOD

"Kaitlyn is only eight, but I think she's already getting breasts. My mother barely talked to me about puberty, and I want her to be better prepared. But why is this happening so soon? I don't think she's ready for it (and neither am I!)."—Petra

Things to Consider

Puberty starts when breast buds start to develop. And it's normal for girls to start puberty over a wide range of ages. Eight is young, but not abnormal. A girl's period will follow within a few years, so you do have time to prepare. There are many excellent books, Web sites, and other resource for both girls and parents. Make use of them to learn as much as you can. The more you both know, the more you can help your daughter understand what's going on and the less apprehension you'll have.

Dads and stepdads usually play more of an emotional supporting role for moms and daughters in these issues. But they need to be well read in the medical and emotional aspects of puberty and be comfortable and accepting of the changes in their daughters' bodies as they are happening. It's important to be unembarrassed to be part of the conversations as long as your daughter welcomes that. Let her know you're not disgusted by women having their period. If she seems to want to talk only to women about these things, respect her need for privacy. She'll let you know when she's comfortable talking about it with you. If you're a single father and she avoids talking with you about this, ask a woman relative or close friend to create a safe relationship with her about it before she's eight.

What to Say and Do

1–7 YEARS OLD

Mom, let her be familiar with your body and be willing to answer all her questions about it.

- You'll grow breasts when you get older.

- That's called pubic hair.

Don't hide signs of your period; talk about it openly and matter-of-factly. Let her wear a menstrual pad when you have your period if she wants to imitate you.

- I have my period every month. It's normal.

- It might look scary, but it doesn't hurt when the blood comes out.

- Those are tampons. They absorb the blood so it doesn't get on my clothes.

8–13 YEARS OLD

Share age-appropriate books, videos, and other materials with her regularly. She'll absorb different information at different ages, so offer the same information many times.

- This is what happens to your body as you become a woman.

Observe the changes that start to happen in her body and emotions and help her understand them. Ask her doctor to talk with you and her about them also. Show her the supplies she'll need and give her her own.

- Your breasts are starting to grow. How do they feel?

- Along with your body changing, your moods and feelings change too.

- Here's a box of pads for you to keep in your bathroom.

- You can carry a pad in your backpack in case your period comes when you're not home.

Talk about your first period if she's interested. Ask how she'd like to celebrate her first period. If she wants it to be very private, respect that.

14 AND UP
If she's concerned about not starting her period yet, reassure her it's normal, and check in with her doctor to confirm there are no health issues.

- Even though it's normal, I understand that you feel different from your friends since you haven't gotten your period. I got mine when I was fifteen.

Words and Phrases to Use

- Healthy

- Normal

- Special

- Growing up

What Not to Say and Do

Don't ignore it or act shocked when she gets her first period.

Don't act frightened or worried when you talk with her about it.

Don't say having your period is disgusting or dirty.

Don't say or imply there's something wrong with her.

Don't refuse to answer her questions or avoid talking about puberty and periods. Don't say,

- You'll learn about that in school.

- Don't ask me. I can't talk about it.

- I don't know.

Words and Phrases to Avoid

- It's gross.

- You're dirty.

- Filthy

- A burden

- On the rag

- Don't tell anyone.

- You shouldn't talk about it.

- Never let a boy know.

Resources

Body Language: New Moon Talks About Growing Up by New Moon Girls Editorial Board. New Moon Publishing, 2004. Available at www.newmoon.org

Growing Up: It's a Girl Thing: Straight Talk about First Bras, First Periods, and Your Changing Body by Mavis Jukes, illustrated by Debbie Tilley. Knopf, 1998.

Our Bodies, Ourselves for the New Century: A Book by and for Women by Boston Women's Health Book Collective. Simon & Schuster, 1998.

Period Book: Everything You Don't Want to Ask (but Need to Know) Karen Gravelle, Debbie Palen, and Jennifer Gravelle. Walker & Co, 1996.

"What's Happening to My Body?" Book for Girls: A Growing-Up Guide for Parents and Daughters by Lynda Madaras, with Area Madaras. Newmarket Press, 2000.

RESPONSIBILITY

"I fear Pam is irresponsible for her age. She forgets to bring her books home, so we have to drive to the school for them or else she can't do her homework. She leaves things lying around the house even though we're always reminding her. She just doesn't seem to see herself as responsible."—Stan

Things to Consider

Responsibility is something girls learn gradually, gaining skills and abilities as they get older. We need to give them opportunities to take on age-appropriate responsibility and experience the logical consequences when they don't fulfill a responsibility. It's important not to give her responsibilities that she's too young for. Then she may become over-responsible and miss out on some of the valuable experiences of childhood.

What to Say and Do

1–7 YEARS OLD
Recognize it when she is responsible in small ways.

- You took very good care of the fish by feeding it every day this week.

- Thanks for helping with the laundry by matching the socks.

- You carried your dishes over to the dishwasher.

8–13 YEARS OLD

Give her age-appropriate responsibilities, increasing them as she gets older.

- Now that you're ten, you can help cook dinner one night a week.

- You can ride the city bus by yourself at twelve.

Give her privileges that match and reward her responsible behavior.

- You're been very responsible with your old bike, so we got you the mountain bike you wanted for Christmas.

- You've learned to handle things at home well, so we can stop doing after-school day care if you feel ready.

14 AND UP

Let go and be clear about the responsibilities you expect her to take on at various ages.

- You're in high school and the optional classes you take are up to you. I'll tell you my opinions, but the decisions are yours.

- I trust you to be responsible with having your friends here.

Let her know the value of doing what she says she will.

- Before you make a promise, think about how realistic it is for you to do it.

- You are someone people know they can rely on to do a good job.

Words and Phrases to Use

- Reliability
- Count on you
- Keep promises.
- Do what you think is right.

- Do it well.
- Follow-through
- Do your best.

What Not to Say and Do

Don't overprotect her from natural consequences of irresponsible behavior. Don't say,

- Your room was so messy I picked it up.

- Since it's so late, I'll look this up for you on the Internet so you can do the worksheet.

Don't accept her blaming others for her irresponsibility. Don't say,

- The coach was mean to bench you; you weren't that late.

- What did the teacher expect you to do?

Words and Phrases to Avoid

- Don't worry about it.

- It's not your fault.

- I can fix it for you.

- I'll take care of it.

Resources

Kids Are Worth It! Revised Edition: Giving Your Child the Gift of Inner Discipline by Barbara Coloroso. HarperCollins, 2002.

Parenting toward Solutions: How to Raise Responsible, Loving Kids by Linda Metcalf. Barnes & Noble Books, 2000.

RISK TAKING

"Sumita is careful about everything. She likes to have a lot of control and isn't very confident. I don't want her to take foolish risks, but I think her life will be boring if she's afraid to take any risks."—Tacia

Things to Consider

The thought of a daughter doing things that may hurt her physically or emotionally is scary to every parent. Our natural desire is to protect our daughters from all possible risks and control situations as much as we can to prevent possible hurt. At the same time, we know that life is full of risks, big and small, and that we need to help our daughters learn how to assess them and cope with them. You won't always be there to protect your girl, and you'll want to know you can rely on her judgment as she gets older.

The old stereotype of girls being "naturally cautious" while boys "run wild" is disappearing. But many parents still find ourselves wanting to protect daughters more than sons from any kind of risk taking, and many girls seem to be afraid of taking risks. We need to work against these instincts for her ultimate benefit. While allowing foolish risk taking is irresponsible, allowing and encouraging her to challenge and stretch herself through age-appropriate risks helps your daughter to develop new abilities through experience.

There's no substitute for learning by doing: it opens up possibilities and expands her horizons. It will help her feel confident about her ability to reach her goals and cope with the unexpected later on in life. It also helps her to develop a strong inner common sense that she can rely on as she becomes more and more independent. And as anyone who's done it knows, taking a risk that doesn't work out the way we wanted it to can teach us things we wouldn't learn any other way.

What to Say and Do

1–7 YEARS OLD
Be encouraging when she takes reasonable risks at any age.

- Look what you did. I'm proud of you!
- You did that even though it was scary. You're brave.

8–13 YEARS OLD
Create clear boundaries for age-appropriate risks, taking her individual capabilities into account. Reassure her that she is capable of doing things she's not done before.

- Remember when you learned to ride your bike?
- I think you can do it.
- I remember how scared I was the first time I sang a solo in choir.

14 AND UP
Encourage her to set goals.

- You can go camping alone with your friends after you have first aid certification.
- When you set your mind to it, you can do anything.

Help her listen to her common sense when assessing risks.

- Does that feel scary to you? Why do you think it does?
- Is there a different way you could try to do it?

Help her think about it when a risk doesn't work out.

- What do you think happened?

- Are there things you would do differently next time?

Words and Phrases to Use

- Give it a try.

- Brave

- Courage

- Good planning

- Weigh the risk.

- Nothing ventured, nothing gained.

- Think it through.

- How will you cope if it doesn't go as planned?

What Not to Say and Do

Don't discourage her from taking age-appropriate risks. Don't say,

- You could kill yourself doing that!

- Are you crazy?

Don't force her to take risks she's unwilling to take. Don't say,

- You have to. Stop stalling!

Don't ignore it if she's feeling scared of doing something. Don't say,

- You're just a scaredy-cat.

- What are you worried about?

Words and Phrases to Avoid

- Where's your brain?

- It's not worth it.

- Just do what you know you can.

- Foolish

- Better safe than sorry.

- I don't think you can handle it.

Resources

Adventures and Challenges: Real Life Stories by Girls and Young Women by Carol Ann Strip and Suzanne M. Bean. Great Potential Press, 1999.

Girls to the Rescue series by Bruce Lansky, published by Meadowbrook Press.

Girls Who Grew Up Great: A Book of Encouragement for Girls about Amazing Women Who Dared to Dream by Gwendolyn Gray. Blue Mountain Arts, 2003.

Risk It! Empowering Young People to Become Positive Risk Takers in the Classroom and in Life by Cathy Newton. Incentive Publications, 1999.

The Romance of Risk: Why Teenagers Do the Things They Do by Lynn E. Ponton. Perseus, 1998.

Self-Direction: Taking Positive Risks, Following Your Dreams by Robert Wandberg. Capstone Press, 2000.

Strong, Smart, and Bold: Empowering Girls for Life by Carla Fine. HarperCollins, 2001.

SCHOOL AND COLLEGE

"School and college are so important today. I want Brenda to do her best. I don't want to pressure her too much, but I think this is one of the most important things for her."—Bradford

Things to Consider

Girls generally like school and perform well in the elementary years. But many girls experience a drop in academic interest by middle school, with all the social issues that come up and pressures for girls to not seem "too smart." Fortunately, schools and teachers are aware of these issues and are working to keep girls interested and rewarded by academics in middle school. Parents play a big role in their success, too. For some girls and families homeschooling can be the best fit. There are more and more resources available to help.

What to Say and Do

1–7 YEARS OLD
Share your daughter's excitement about school. Let her express her frustrations about it, too.

- I'm so glad you like school.

- What did you work on today?

- That sounds frustrating; tell me about it.

8–13 YEARS OLD

Help her develop her own best way of studying.

- It seems like you can concentrate best before dinner.

- I've noticed you like to talk about your ideas before you write them down. I like to hear about them.

Encourage her to take a variety of subjects.

- Trying things to see what you like is the whole point of all the classes that are offered.

If she's having trouble with a particular class, ask her about it.

- That's giving you a challenge. What do you think might help? Let's talk with your teacher about it.

Advocate with her teachers to work with her personal learning style.

14 AND UP

Give her full responsibility for managing her homework. If her grades decline, consider whether nonacademic issues might be the cause.

- It's unusual for your grades to go down. Why do you think they did?

When it's time to start thinking about choosing a college, let her take the lead.

- We can go look at some colleges this spring. Where would you like to visit?

- What are you interested in in a college?

- It's a big decision. I have a lot of confidence in you making a good choice.

If she doesn't get accepted at her top choices, help her cope with the disappointment.

- I didn't get into the college I really wanted to go to. But the place I went turned out to be really great for me, probably even better than my first choice.

- It's possible to transfer into a school after one or two years somewhere else.

Words and Phrases to Use

- Learning
- Opportunity
- Variety
- Choice

- Follow your interests.
- What do you want to know?
- You're a good student.
- You work hard.

What Not to Say and Do

Don't equate her academic success with her value as a person. Don't say,

- It's a good thing you're so smart.
- When you get a B, that's very disappointing.

Don't pressure her to choose the college you think will be best. Don't say,

- Why aren't you applying to any competitive schools?
- I know this is the best place for you.
- You don't know how to pick a college and I do.
- We're paying for it, so you need to listen to what we want.

Words and Phrases to Avoid

- The only way

- Dumb

- Stupid

- Underachiever

- I know best.

Resources

All Girls: Single-Sex Education and Why It Matters by Karen Stabiner. Riverhead, 2002.

Failing at Fairness: How Our Schools Cheat Girls by Myra and David Sadker. Simon & Schuster, 1995.

Girls' Guide to the SAT: Tips and Techniques for Closing the Gender Gap by Alexandra Freer and Nancy C. Redding. Random House, 2003.

Guerrilla Learning: How to Give Your Kids a Real Education with or without School by Grace Llewellyn and Amy Silverman. John Wiley & Sons, 2001.

Homeschooling: The Teen Years: Your Guide to Successfully Homeschooling the 13- to 18-Year-Old by Cafi Cohen. Crown Publishing, 2000.

Laughing Allegra: The Inspiring Story of a Mother's Struggle and Triumph Raising a Daughter with Learning Disabilities by Anne Ford. Newmarket Press, 2003.

Schoolgirls: Young Women, Self-Esteem, and the Confidence Gap by Peggy Orenstein. Doubleday, 1994.

A Sense of Self: Listening to Homeschooled Adolescent Girls by Susannah Sheffer. Heinemann, 1996.

Teenage Liberation Handbook: How to Quit School and Get a Real Life and Education by Grace Llewellyn. Lowry House, 1998.

American Association of University Women: www.aauw.org (has wide-ranging resources and reports on girls and school)

Growing without Schooling: www.holtgws.com

National Coalition of Girls Schools: www.ncgs.org

SCIENCE AND MATH

"Erika has a talent for science and math. She loves them, too. I know that girls often lose interest in these subjects in middle school—that happened to me. What can I do to keep it from happening to her?"—Maggie

Things to Consider

Science and math are important for *everyone* in our highly technological society, not just those who want to follow a career in those areas. But let's face it; the career choices open to people in these fields usually pay pretty well, too. And much of the job growth predicted in the future is in scientific and technological fields. Considering all this, it's definitely worth nurturing your daughter's interest in science and math. It's also worth nurturing for the sheer joy she can experience in learning these ways of thinking and exploring the world.

Parents can make a big difference in girls' continued interest in science and math. We can give them science kits and books on physics and help them conduct their own experiments at home as part of their daily routine. To do this, we might need to let go of our own feelings of inferiority and intimidation about science and math. It can be liberating for us and for them!

What to Say and Do

1–7 YEARS OLD

Kids are natural scientists, using observation and experimentation in everyday life. Recognize this as science and talk about her experiments.

- You're a scientist experimenting with what floats in the tub.

- You noticed that the cardinals like to go to one feeder more than the other. Why do you think that is?

Give her toys at all ages that use science and math.

8–13 YEARS OLD

When she asks a question that could be answered by doing an experiment, help her do that instead of just telling her the answer. Emphasize the fun of solving the mystery.

- I'm not sure what would happen if we move this plant away from the window. What do you think? Let's leave one at the window and move one away and see if they react differently.

- It's a mystery to me why one recipe has yeast and one doesn't but they both rise. Let's read about the chemistry of it.

Play math-based games like cards and dominoes. Use math concepts like percentages, ratios, and geometric progressions when discussing nonmath things that she has a strong interest in.

Learn science and math with her if you're rusty at them or didn't take what she's taking. She'll love to explain things to you and be your teacher.

Notice what specific aspects of science and math interest her and provide more opportunities in those.

- There's a junior naturalist program in the park this summer.

- You and your friends are being psychologists when you notice how people act and come up with theories about why.

If her interest in math and science classes seems to be dropping, talk with her teachers and the school right away. Be assertive about the need for keeping her interested. Consider tutoring if you and the teacher think that would help.

14 AND UP
Encourage her to take math and science all the way through high school.

- It gives you so many options when you get to college.

- I know chemistry isn't your favorite class and you're glad it's almost done. Physics is very different from chemistry, and I think you'll like it a lot. I'd like you to try it next year.

- You have a gift for geometry; I think it's part of your interest in architecture.

Camps can provide science experiences in a fun environment.

Search out intern/volunteer opportunities for her to use science and math.

Words and Phrases to Use

- Scientist
- Curious
- Mystery
- Detective
- Formula

- Experiment
- Theories
- Research
- Results
- Hypothesis

What Not to Say and Do

Don't dwell on how you're "terrible in math and science." Don't say,

- I could never do that stuff. It's too hard.

- Women just don't like those subjects. They're so impersonal.

Don't let her put down her own abilities in science and math. Don't say,

■ You're right. You've never been good at math.

■ I guess you just don't have a science mind.

Words and Phrases to Avoid

■ Science is boring.

■ I'm math impaired.

■ I can't even balance the checkbook.

■ That's just for brilliant people.

■ Geeky

■ Antisocial

Resources

365 Super Science Experiments with Everyday Materials by E. Richard Churchill, Muriel Mandell, Frances Zweifel, and Louis V. Loeschnig. Sterling Publishing, 2001.

The Math Book for Girls and Other Beings Who Count by Valerie Wyatt. Kids Can Press, 2000.

The Science Education of American Girls by Kim Tolley. Taylor & Francis, 2002.

The Ultimate Girl's Guide to Science: From Backyard Experiments to Winning the Nobel Prize! by Erica Ritter. Beyond Words Publishing, 2004.

Girl Start: www.girlstart.org

SECURITY AND SAFETY

"Of course I want to keep my daughter safe and secure. It was easy to do that when she was little. But now that she's getting older, how do I protect her without making her and us paranoid? I want her to feel secure, not frightened of things."—Asok

Things to Consider

When our daughters are small, we can make them feel safe and secure just by being there. They trust us to keep the world safe for them, and for the most part we feel we can do it. But how can we protect them when we're not there? As they start to venture out past our families, they need to be able to carry their sense of security and safety with them.

A girl needs to develop a good sense of what situations she can handle and what she can't. She needs to learn basic safety rules and first aid. She also needs to develop some "street smarts" so she can assess circumstances, think on her feet, and take action to protect herself. She can learn these skills by being exposed to age-appropriate situations where she needs to figure out how to cope on her own without our intervention. Doing this develops her skill and also her confidence, which is a key part of safety and security.

What to Say and Do

1–7 YEARS OLD

Teach her basic safety skills like what to do in a fire or if she gets lost.

- If we're at the store and you can't find me, what do you need to do?

- What would you do if there was a fire in the kitchen?

8–13 YEARS OLD

Allow her to get experience in situations where she makes some safety/security decisions for herself. Talk with her about possible situations.

- Now that you know the safe biking rules, you can ride to school by yourself.

- What would you do if you were walking down the street and a car pulled over next to you?

Give her helpful feedback on her decisions.

- You handled it very well when the dog ran into the street. It wouldn't have been safe to follow her into the traffic even though you were worried about her getting hit.

Get her training in first aid and self-defense.

- Knowing these things means you can handle more situations without me there.

- Listen to your intuition about whether a situation or person is safe or not. Intuition is a great tool.

14 AND UP

Let her know her safety and security are important to you.

- The rule we have about not driving with more than one friend is for your safety.

Tell her you trust her to take care of her own safety and security.

- You've shown us that you make good decisions about safety.

Accept that you can't protect her from everything.

Words and Phrases to Use

- Safeguard
- Care
- Intuition
- Trust your gut.

- Awareness
- Alert
- Paying attention
- Thinking ahead

What Not to Say and Do

Don't talk so much about your fears that she takes them on. Don't say,

- The world isn't safe for girls.
- Every time you go out, I'm a nervous wreck until you're home again.
- It's not absolutely safe, so you can't do it.

Don't ignore the fact that there are safety and security issues for her. Don't say,

- You don't have anything to worry about.
- Do whatever you want. It'll be fine.

Words and Phrases to Avoid

- There's danger everywhere.

- You can't trust anyone.

- You can only depend on your family.

Resources

A Girl's Gotta Do What a Girl's Gotta Do: The Safety Chick's Guide to Living Safe and Smart by Kathleen Baty. Rodale Press, 2003.

Predators: Pedophiles, Rapists, and Other Sex Offenders: Who They Are, How They Operate, and How We Can Protect Ourselves and Our Children by Anna C. Salter. Basic Books, 2003.

Protecting the Gift: Keeping Children and Teenagers Safe and Parents Sane by Gavin de Becker. Dell, 2000.

Self-Defense and Assault Prevention for Girls and Women by Bruce Tegner. Thor Publishing, 1997.

SELF-ESTEEM AND SELF-ACCEPTANCE

"Charisse has a bit of a self-esteem problem. When things go wrong, she gets down on herself and blames herself. I don't want her to be a braggart, but I want her to feel better. I tell her all the time how good she is and I try to praise her a lot. It doesn't seem to make any difference. What am I doing wrong?"—Darrell

Things to Consider

Self-esteem is a realistic valuing and acceptance of herself, not an inflated fantasy. Strong self-esteem can be your daughter's best defense during the tumultuous teen years, and self-esteem and self-respect are closely related. Girls who genuinely value and respect themselves are much more likely to value and respect others.

So how do we give her self-esteem and self-acceptance? In the most basic sense, we can't. Self-esteem is what she thinks of herself, and it grows out of her experiences and the feedback she gets from them. We can give her all the praise in the world and it won't give her positive self-esteem. And while we can give her a good start by taking care of her and treating her with respect, we can't build her self-esteem for her.

One thing we *can* do is pay attention to our own self-esteem. How well do we honestly value and respect ourselves? Strengthening our own self-esteem will help our daughters. Self-acceptance is the process of knowing our strengths and weaknesses and accepting them both. We can help girls with this by acknowledging their weaknesses along with their strengths, and showing them we love them just the same.

What to Say and Do

1–7 YEARS OLD
Consistently meet a girl's true physical and emotional needs and provide strong guidance as she develops.

- You're important to me because you're you.

- Taking care of yourself makes you strong.

- Learning new things makes you feel good.

- I love you.

8–13 YEARS OLD
Give her many opportunities to learn and do things. Developing skills and finding out what she's good at builds self-esteem.

Self-acceptance comes from knowing she doesn't have to be good at everything.

- You're very good at chess and not so good at gymnastics.

- We all have some things we're good at and some things we're awful at. That's human.

Take her seriously and listen to her with an open mind.

- What you say is important to me. I'm listening.

- What are you doing when you feel really good about yourself?

Support her in respecting herself by treating her with respect.

- I respect you and your feelings.

- You showed self-respect when you calmly told Marcy it was disloyal to tell your secret to someone else.

- You know how to nurture yourself and take a break when you need it.

If her self-esteem takes a normal dip at puberty, help her understand it happens to other kids, too.

- This is a difficult time for most kids, and it's usual for you to feel a bit less confident. What do you think might help your confidence come back?

14 AND UP

Help her keep exploring and learning more complicated things. Overcoming challenges is also a positive boost to self-esteem.

- Knowing another language is a great skill.

- I'm glad you gave it a try. You picked it up very quickly.

Being part of a group activity where she feels she can contribute is very helpful.

Words and Phrases to Use

- You're a good person.
- I love you.
- Worthwhile
- Your special personal gifts
- Good job.

- You're special to me.
- Well done.
- You know yourself well.
- You're good at that.
- You treat others well.

What Not to Say and Do

Don't give her unrealistic, mindless praise. Don't say,

- You're the best in the world.

- No one's as good as you.

Don't tease her about things she's not good at. Don't say,

- You can't even draw a straight line. Some artist you are.

- That's a good laugh—a klutz like you trying out for softball.

Words and Phrases to Avoid

- What a loser.

- Can't you do anything right?

- Why bother?

- You'll never learn.

- Why can't you be like your sister?

- Everyone else in our family is athletic but you.

- Just mediocre

- If you tried harder, you could do it.

Resources

200 Ways to Raise a Girl's Self-Esteem by Will Glennon. Red Wheel/Weiser, 1999.

Free to Be . . . You and Me by Marlo Thomas. Running Press, 2002.

Girls on Track: A Parent's Guide to Inspiring Our Daughters to Achieve a Lifetime of Self-Esteem and Respect by Molly Barker. Ballantine Books, 2004.

Nurturing Good Children Now by Ron Taffel. St. Martin's Press, 2000.

Ophelia Speaks: Adolescent Girls Write about Their Search for Self by Sara Shandler. HarperCollins, 1999.

SEXUAL IDENTITY

"Sarah is fourteen and has a very close friend whom she spends nearly all her time with. I think they have romantic feelings for each other. I have mixed feelings about this. I want Sarah to be happy, and if she's a lesbian, I don't want her to deny that. But I worry about others' prejudices toward homosexuals. Does a fourteen-year-old have a definite sexual identity, or could she be experimenting?"—Denise

Things to Consider

It's not uncommon for a girl to have sexual feelings for or crushes on another girl, even if she isn't homosexual. And some of our daughters will grow up as lesbians or bisexuals. Some lesbian and bisexual adults say they felt different starting at a very young age; others say they weren't aware of their sexual preference until later in adolescence. Some girls do experiment with sexual identity in order to sort out their own confusion. Homosexuality and bisexuality are not illnesses, disorders, or moral failings. The American Psychological and Psychiatric Associations compare them to being left- or right-handed.

Your daughter will probably tell someone else (a friend, counselor, religious leader, her diary) about any same-sex attraction before she tells you. And it will probably be a very confusing time for her if she realizes she's attracted to other girls. Being able to talk openly with you and others about her feelings is very important. A teen's sense of herself as a maturing sexual person is a key part of her overall identity. You may already have had a sense of her sexual identity, or it may be a complete shock. Either way, it can be a tough time for all of you. Don't make it worse by rejecting her or pulling away. A girl discovering that she is lesbian or bisexual needs your support. Listen to her respectfully and don't try to talk her out of it. Let her know you support her. Your acceptance greatly increases her ability to get to know and accept herself in a healthy way.

Show her well before puberty that you are not prejudiced against homosexuals or bisexuals. That way, she's more likely to feel she can talk with you about her feelings and possible confusion. At the same time, watch for the problems she may face. Homosexual teens have higher rates of depression, drinking, smoking, and suicide. Parental support is the best antidote for those problems. Be honest with each other about the difficulties she's likely to face, but don't let them overwhelm your expressions of love and acceptance. As in every other aspect of life, we can't protect our daughters from being who they are or keep them locked up in a tower as they grow up.

If you are homosexual or bisexual, it's likely that you'll have prepared your daughter for open talk about sexual identity since she was young. You may feel somewhat rejected or disappointed if she's heterosexual. The same principles of accepting her and who she is apply in this situation.

What to Say and Do

1–7 YEARS OLD
Treat people respectfully regardless of their sexual preference.

Answer her questions about sexual identity factually and without prejudice.

- Kerry has two dads. They're gay and they love each other romantically like Dad and I do.

8–13 YEARS OLD
Listen carefully and directly answer any questions she asks. These are your cues for the information she needs.

- I'm glad you asked about that. Here's what I think.

Provide books and other sources of information, especially if she's private and doesn't ask you questions.

Describe sexual identity as part of what makes up a whole person but not the most important thing.

- Who we're interested in romantically is part of who we are as a person.
- Some people feel embarrassed talking about sexual preference, but it's a totally natural thing.

14 AND UP

If you think she needs to talk about it but won't talk with you, ask a trusted adult to bring it up with her.

Be ready to listen whenever and wherever she brings the topic up with you. Accept her as who she is.

- Whenever you want to talk about it, I'll be available.
- I'll listen to everything you have to say and not interrupt.
- I love you for yourself.

Watch for warning signs of inner conflict she may have about her sexual identity.

- You and Kym aren't spending any time together lately. Is she uncomfortable since you told her you're a lesbian?
- You have seemed very quiet the past few weeks. I get the feeling there's something on your mind.

Reassure her that confused and strong feelings about sexual identity are normal during adolescence.

- The way you're feeling is completely normal. Your body and mind and feelings are going through a lot of changes, and it takes a while for it to all get settled down.
- I've felt sexually attracted to other women sometimes. It's OK.

Words and Phrases to Use

- Acceptance
- Love
- Support
- Understanding
- Your true self
- OK
- Who you are

- Homosexual
- Gay
- Lesbian
- Bisexual
- Preference
- Respect

What Not to Say and Do

Don't dismiss her sexual identity as just a phase. Don't say,

- You'll grow out of it.
- You don't know what you want.
- I won't listen to that nonsense.
- Who are you kidding? You're not bisexual.

Don't put the focus on other people's feelings about her sexual identity. Don't say,

- How can you do this to me?
- Your grandparents will be devastated.
- What will your friends think?

Don't make insulting or prejudiced remarks about homosexuals or bisexuals. Don't say,

- Those gay people make me sick.

■ How can they have sex with another woman?

Don't tell jokes that make fun of any sexual identity.

Words and Phrases to Avoid

■ Immoral

■ Gross

■ Abnormal

■ Disgusting

■ Sinful

■ Unnatural

■ Keep it secret.

■ Don't tell anyone.

■ Bad

■ Unhealthy

■ Slutty

■ Dirty

Resources

Changing Bodies, Changing Lives by Ruth Bell. Crown Publishing, 1998.

Free Your Mind: The Book for Gay, Lesbian, and Bisexual Youth—And Their Allies by Ellen Bass and Kate Kaufman. HarperCollins, 1996.

Queer 13: Lesbian and Gay Writers Recall Seventh Grade by Clifford Chase. William Morrow, 1999.

The Secret a Child Dare Not Tell by Mary Ann Cantwell. Rafael Press, 1996.

Gay, Lesbian and Straight Education Network: www.glsen.org

Parents, Families and Friends of Lesbians and Gays: www.pflag.org

SEXUALITY

"I don't know how to talk to Shakira about sex. I want her to know that it can be loving and wonderful and fulfilling. But I'm a very private person and just can't imagine talking with my daughter about this. And being her dad, I think she'd be embarrassed if I brought it up. Is it better for her mom to just handle it all?"—Gary

Things to Consider

For many parents, the thought of talking about sex and sexuality with our daughters is scary. Sex is about sharing the deepest intimacy, and most of us were raised by parents who gave us "just the facts"—if that. We probably learned much of what we know from our peers, the media, our good and bad experiences, and books. We need to decide if we want our daughters to learn about their sexuality the same way and have similar confusion and uncertainty. If not, we need to gather up our courage, prepare ourselves, and talk about it with them regularly as they are growing up.

It *is* possible to talk with a girl about sex without being intrusive or inappropriate. By helping your daughter learn and talk within your family about both her sexuality and sex itself, you prepare her to have positive experiences and a healthy perspective about the role of sex in relationships. The consequences of having sex can be just as life changing as those of a car crash. We'd never let our daughters just drive out on the highway without extensive teaching and practicing their skills. Why would we let her approach sex less prepared?

All that said, mothers and fathers often have different roles in teaching girls about sex and sexuality. By treating information about sex as a normal subject of family communication when a girl's young, parents create an atmosphere where she feels that she can ask anything of either parent. But it's important to maintain healthy boundaries when we talk about sex with our daughters. It's not healthy for parents to discuss their sexual relationship in detail with girls or in front of them. The conversation should meet their needs for information, not our emotional needs.

As your daughter gets older, she may start limiting those conversations to Mom only. Follow her lead and let her choose who she wants to talk with about it. Dad and Mom can still talk with each other matter-of-factly about sex in front of their girl. And Dad can pick opportune moments to tell brief stories that focus on his feelings and confusion about sex as a teen. It's helpful for girls to know that boys feel just as uncertain and confused as they do about sex, even though they may not show it.

What to Say and Do

1–7 YEARS OLD

Let sex and sexuality come up naturally in family conversation and answer her questions. Give her age-appropriate facts and use correct terms for body parts.

- Sex can feel cozy and wonderful.

- Girls have a vagina and clitoris and boys have a penis.

- When people have sex, they are very close and trusting of each other.

8–13 YEARS OLD

Tell her it's normal for girls and women (not just boys and men) to have sexual feelings and desires.

- When I had a crush on someone, I'd feel all tingly in my genitals when I saw them. That's called feeling aroused.

- It feels very special when you're attracted to someone and they're attracted to you.

- I like kissing. I felt guilty about it when I was a teen, but now I know it's a normal feeling.

- Sexual feelings are very powerful.

Stress the importance of mutual respect, choice, and responsibility in a sexual relationship.

- It's up to you to decide if you want to have sex with anyone. You don't have to go along with it if you don't want to. If someone tries to force you, that's wrong.

- When two people care about each other enough to have sex, that's a special thing.

Let her know that people have individual tastes in what they enjoy sexually.

- People don't all like the same things sexually. What you like might change as you grow up.

Masturbation is normal and healthy for girls.

- It's OK to masturbate. It feels good.

Provide her with books, newsletters, and other materials that give accurate, nurturing information about human sexuality including details about sexual organs and sexual response.

14 AND UP

Talk specifically about the risks of intercourse, oral and anal sex, and alternatives for feeling sexually satisfied.

- There are serious health risks in any kind of sex that involves body fluids. Here's information to read and then we'll talk about it.

- You can have an orgasm without intercourse or oral or anal sex.

Let her ask you and tell you anything about sex. Stay calm and listen carefully.

- I'm so glad you're telling me this. I'll respect your trust in me.

- I don't know the answer to your question. Let's look for more information.

- I wonder what's going through your mind about this?

Words and Phrases to Use

- Normal
- Sex
- Sexuality
- Vagina and clitoris
- Penis and testicles
- Healthy

- Think about it.
- Prepare
- Protect yourself.
- Caring
- Mutual feelings

What Not to Say and Do

Don't refuse to answer her questions about sex. Don't say,

- You're too young to ask that.
- We don't talk about that in our family.
- You'll find out for yourself like I did.

Don't tell her girls shouldn't be interested in sex. Don't say,

- Girls who think about sex are sluts.
- Don't act interested in sex; it gives boys the wrong idea.

Don't tell her it's her responsibility to control a boy's behavior. Don't say,

- You must have lead him on.

- Boys have no self-control.

- What did you do to encourage him?

Words and Phrases to Avoid

- Sex is dirty.

- Nasty

- Sinful

- Guilt

- You just have to endure it.

- Immoral

- You'll regret it.

- Decadent

- Unladylike

- Don't ever touch yourself down there.

Resources

All about Sex: A Family Resource on Sex and Sexuality, edited by Ronald Filiberti Moglia and Jon Knowles. Three Rivers Press, 1997.

Everything You Never Wanted Your Kids to Know about Sex (But Were Afraid They'd Ask): The Secrets to Surviving Your Child's Sexual Development from Birth to the Teens by Justin Richardson and Mark Schuster. Crown Publishing, 2003.

How Can We Talk about That? Overcoming Personal Hangups So We Can Teach Kids the Right Stuff about Sex and Morality by Jane DiVita Woody. John Wiley & Sons, 2001.

Sex and Sensibility: The Thinking Parent's Guide to Talking Sense about Sex by Deborah M. Roffman. Perseus, 2001.

SEX, ETC., the newsletter of the National Teen-to-Teen Sexuality Education Project run by the Network for Family Life Education at Rutgers, the State University of New Jersey: www.sxetc.org

Sex Lives of Teenagers: Revealing the Secret World of Adolescent Boys and Girls by Lynn E. Ponton. Plume, 2001.

Ten Talks Parents Must Have with Their Children about Sex and Character by Pepper Schwartz and Dominic Cappello. Hyperion, 2000.

SIBLINGS

"Margaret and her brother fight a lot. They're jealous of each other and competitive. Every now and then they get along well, but those times are few and far between. My sister is one of my good friends, and I want them to have that kind of bond. What's wrong?"—Theo

Things to Consider

Sibling relationships are affected by a lot of factors—a large age difference, clashing personalities, and widely varying interests. Serious sibling conflict can be a wake-up call that one child or the other has behavioral or emotional problems, or that the parents' marriage or overall family dynamics (favoritism of one child, for instance) are an issue. But if you've explored those possibilities and they're not the cause, communicating with your kids about their animosity can make the difference.

Even if your daughter has traditionally had a close relationship with her siblings, she will probably still have times of conflict and distancing from them as she goes through adolescence. That's normal. Particularly in later adolescence, she has to prepare to separate from them as well as from you. Sometimes creating conflict is how she handles that.

What to Say and Do

1–7 YEARS OLD
Teach her to respect her siblings and play fair.

- You know Stevie doesn't like it when you do that. Please stop now.

- Amy does it her way and you do it yours. That's OK.

- Taking turns is the fair way.

8–13 YEARS OLD
Value each sibling for who they are.

- You and Mercy are very different. I love you both so much.

- I really enjoy seeing you have fun with your brother.

- You can fight and still forgive each other and love each other.

Create special times together for her and her siblings to remember later.

- Remember when we were camping and the tent fell down in the night?

14 AND UP
Understand that sibling conflict now may be part of her emotional separation from the family.

- I know your sister is getting on your nerves. This is a big transition time for both of you. Some conflict is normal. It will get better again.

Words and Phrases to Use

- Love
- Caring

- Connection
- Family

- Sharing
- Fun

- Special relationship

What Not to Say and Do

Don't give her unreasonable responsibility for younger siblings. Don't say,

- You can't go to the party. You have to babysit.
- You help other people but never me.
- Why did you let him do that?

Don't treat siblings unfairly. Don't say,

- Your brother is my favorite. You know that.
- She's younger than you and needs all my attention.

Don't pit siblings against each other.

- I like her better.
- Why can't you be more like him?
- Why do you hate your sister?

Resources

Loving Each One Best: A Caring and Practical Approach to Raising Siblings by Nancy Samalin and Catherine Whitney. Bantam, 1996.

"Mom, Jason's Breathing on Me!" The Solution to Sibling Bickering by Anthony Wolf. Random House, 2003.

Siblings without Rivalry by Adele Faber and Elaine Mazlish. HarperCollins, 1998.

Sisters, written and illustrated by David McPhail. Harcourt Brace, 2003.

SLEEP

"Sleep has been an issue for Mercedes most of her life. She needs more than most kids her age, but she hates to miss out on things and has trouble relaxing when it's bedtime. I'm actually looking forward to her being a teenager and wanting to sleep!"—Tallulah

Things to Consider

When they're little, children are guided by their body's need for sleep as long as emotional or physical issues don't disrupt them. Developing a consistent nap and bedtime schedule and a relaxing presleep routine are very helpful. Don't turn it into a power struggle, but let her know that when you say it's time for a nap or bed, it's time.

Once she's school age, outside activities can create more desire to stay up later and not get enough sleep. You need to be tuned in to your daughter's individual sleep needs and set the boundaries that will keep her healthy.

Once she's a teen, her need for sleep is actually greater than in the preteen years. A minimum of nine hours a night is needed to give her body and brain the time to grow, recharge, and process the experiences of the day. At the same time, her inner body clock is changing and it's hard for her to fall asleep as early as she used to. Many teenagers are wide awake until midnight or later and have great difficulty being alert in the early morning, no matter how much sleep they've had. This is biology and not laziness. But most high schools start as early as 7:15 a.m. Then, after-school and social activities take place in the afternoon and evening. Given all these factors, it's hard to know how to help your daughter get the sleep she needs for her physical and emotional health. Talk with other parents and her school about starting later or try to arrange her schedule for less challenging classes in the early morning.

What to Say and Do

1–7 YEARS OLD

Create a consistent presleep routine that helps her relax and that she can gradually do for herself as she gets older.

- It's almost bedtime, so get on your jammies and we'll read two stories in your bed.

- Now we'll turn the light off and I'll give you a short back rub.

Bad dreams and other sleep disturbances are common at these ages. Soothe her and help her learn to soothe herself back to sleep.

8–13 YEARS OLD

Teach her self-relaxation techniques she can use on her own.

- I'll help you practice the relaxing breathing when you get into bed.

- Pachelbel's "Canon" is relaxing music to listen to while you fall asleep.

Pay attention to signs that she's not getting enough sleep and talk with her about them.

- You've fallen asleep watching a video the past few nights after dinner. That tells me you're not getting enough sleep and we need to change that.

- I've noticed that when you go to bed by 8:30, you wake up easily without the alarm the next morning.

- We can try having you set your own bedtime for a week, and then we'll talk about how it's going.

14 AND UP

Help her take on the awareness and responsibility for how much sleep she needs and gets.

- I know being in the play is really important to you, but you've been so tired since rehearsals started. How about coming home for a quick snooze in the afternoons?

- I've read that teenagers need at least nine hours of sleep a night, but you mostly get seven. I wonder how it affects your mood when you feel tired all the time.

- Since you feel sharper mentally after 11 a.m., let's see about scheduling your math and science classes after then.

- Even if you're not sleeping, resting with your eyes closed or listening to quiet music helps your body recharge.

Let her sleep as much as she wants on holidays and weekends.

- You can sleep in on Saturday and Sunday; it's good to see you feeling rested when you get up.

- Tell me if you want to be up by a certain time; otherwise I'll let you sleep.

Words and Phrases to Use

- Body clock

- Relaxation

- Rest

- Sleep helps you grow.

- Some people need more sleep than others.

- How do you feel?

- What do you think?

- How can you feel more rested?

What Not to Say and Do

Don't ignore her personal sleep needs or assume they are the same as yours. Don't say,

- I just wake up naturally at 5:30 every morning. I don't know what's the matter with you.

- You need ten hours of sleep every night. That's what I needed at your age.

Don't turn it into a power struggle. Don't say,

- It doesn't matter what you think. I told you it's bedtime.

- I don't care if you're not tired. Go to bed.

Words and Phrases to Avoid

- Just do what I say.

- You have to get up at the same time every day.

- You're just lazy.

- No one should need to sleep that late.

SPORTS AND PHYSICAL ACTIVITY

"My daughter's quite a couch potato. We'd like to get her more active and know that sports have a lot of benefits, but she says she doesn't like the competitiveness. Should we make her try some sports anyway?"—Hiroki

Things to Consider

There's so much research showing how sports can be beneficial for girls, both physically and psychologically. But that's only if she's a willing participant. Being forced by you isn't going to create a good experience. There are many other ways she can be physically active, and you can find something she will like to do—whether it's dancing or hiking or backyard badminton or yoga or tai chi. The important thing is getting her regularly moving her body and learning its strengths and capabilities. Being active together is a great stress reliever and a fun way to increase family time.

If your daughter *is* interested in sports, there are several things parents should be aware of. Regardless of how athletically talented she is (or is not), she can feel good about doing sports when she has the right team and coach for her. She might prefer an individual sport where she can better her skills one on one. Learning how to be a good sport—how to play hard, support the team, lose gracefully, and put a defeat behind her—is valuable. Be sure the situation she's in is matched to her individual desire for competition and challenge.

What to Say and Do

1–7 YEARS OLD
Do what's fun for her.

- Want to play tag?

- How about going swimming?

Any team she's on should be loosely organized and focused completely on fun.

8–13 YEARS OLD
Let her try as many sports and activities as she wants to.

If she's really committed to team sports, let her do one at a time and support her team.

- You can do soccer in the fall and softball in the summer.

- I'll volunteer to be assistant coach this year.

Do noncompetitive activities as a family, at home and on vacation.

- We're all going on a bike ride this afternoon.

If she loses interest in something she used to love, ask why.

- Was there something about the team or the coach that changed?

14 AND UP
This is when many girls give up team sports for other interests. Help her stay involved if you can but don't force it. Help her find a new physical activity if she stops doing a sport.

- Is there anything I can do to help you stay with soccer?

- I saw there's an Irish dancing class starting next month.

- Jogging is something you can do at your pace.

Words and Phrases to Use

- Fun
- Active
- Teamwork
- Good sport
- Improving
- Relaxing

- De-stressing
- Doing your best
- Feels good
- Feeling strong
- Doing your part

What Not to Say and Do

Don't overemphasize the competitive aspect of sports. Don't say,

- Winning is what matters most.
- No one likes a loser.
- There's only one winner.

Don't discourage her from physical activity. Don't say,

- That's not ladylike.
- You don't want to get sweaty.
- It's messy.
- It's too hard for you.
- You can't do it.
- You're uncoordinated.

Actions to Avoid

- Don't yell at her from the sidelines.

- Don't insult the referees.

- Avoid being rude to fans for the opposing team.

- Don't say, "Kill 'em."

- Don't say, "Hurt 'em."

- Never intervene in a game.

Resources

Body Thieves: Help Girls Reclaim Their Natural Bodies and Become Physically Active by Sandra S. Friedman. Salal Books, 2002.

Catch Them Being Good: Everything You Need to Know to Successfully Coach Girls by Tony Dicicco, Charles Salzberg, and Colleen Hacker. Viking, 2002.

Mistakes Worth Making: How to Turn Sports Errors into Athletic Excellence by Susan Halden-Brown. Human Kinetics, 2002.

New Moon Sports by the Girls Editorial Board, 1999. (more information at www.new-moon.org)

Raising Our Athletic Daughters by Jean Simmerman and Gil Reavill. Doubleday, 1998.

Women's Sports Foundation: www.womenssportsfoundation.org

SEXUALLY TRANSMITTED DISEASES

*"I don't even want to think about the risks kids face today from sexually trans-
mitted diseases. How do I tell her about them so she understands the risks and
doesn't just turn a deaf ear to what I'm saying?"—Robert*

Things to Consider

STDs are a major health risk for sexually active teens. Many of them are life threatening like HIV (which causes AIDS) and hepatitis and cannot be cured (even with treatment) once you have them. Many STDs are silent. They don't show up immediately,
and unless someone has been tested since their last unprotected sex, he or she won't
even know they have the disease. Most teens have dangerously limited knowledge
about STDs and how to protect against them. That lack of knowledge can affect them
for the rest of their lives if they have unprotected sex with an infected person.

Regardless of how you feel about teens having sex, it's wise to be sure your daughter is fully informed about STDs, prevention, and symptoms. The reality is that most girls
have intercourse before they are eighteen. Parents have to deal realistically with the very
real possibility that their daughter might be one of them. Start by informing yourself and

reading suggestions on how to present the facts most effectively to your daughter. If you think she didn't really listen to you, enlist another person to talk with her about this and give her a lot of reading material and Web sites to look at.

What to Say and Do

12 AND UP
When you talk with her about sex, mention STDs as part of what she needs to know.

- One of the things about sex that's not pleasant is STDs.

- Do you know what STDs are?

- The only way to totally prevent getting an STD is not having sex.

- All sex must be protected sex, including oral sex.

- Condoms are the only protection against STDs, but they're not 100 percent effective.

- Other kinds of birth control (like the pill or foam) don't protect you from STDs.

Be sure she's vaccinated against all STDs there are vaccines for. Check with her doctor about what's available.

If she has unprotected sex, get her tested for STDs.

- The sooner you get the tests, the better the chances of treatment are.

Tell her she can ask you anything. Answer her questions calmly and factually.

Tell her you'll support and help her if she has a problem.

- We'll always be there for you if you need us.

Words and Phrases to Use

- STDs are serious.

- You can protect yourself from STDs.

- Here's something I want you to read.

- Safe sex

- HIV

- AIDS

- Chlamydia

- Condom

- Herpes

- Hepatitis B and C

What Not to Say and Do

Don't neglect to talk about STDs. Don't say,

- All you need to know is that if you don't have sex, you'll be safe.

Don't say or imply that STDs are a punishment. Don't say,

- It's God's punishment for immorality.

- Gay men deserve AIDS.

Words and Phrases to Avoid

- That's what you get.

- You're a slut.

- You're immoral.

- I told you to watch out.

Resources

Sexually Transmitted Diseases by Tassia Kolesnikow. Gale Group, 2003.

I Wanna Know: www.iwannaknow.org

Planned Parenthood: www.ppfa.org

STRESS

"Kids have such stressful lives today. Between school and activities, they never have a moment to breathe. And the rest of the world is a stressful place right now, with terrorism and all the bad news we hear about every day. My husband and I are stressed about it all, and we're adults. How can we help our daughter cope with all this?"—Lorinda

Things to Consider

Stress is a fact of life, and learning to recognize and manage it is one of the most useful skills we can give our daughters. They'll learn first from watching how we manage (or don't manage) our stress.

Even so, kids can often teach us something about coping with stress. Working it out physically comes naturally to kids and is one of the best approaches. Running is a fantastic stress reliever and young girls do it often. We can take a cue from them and include more exercise in everyday life. Talking and creative self-expression are also wonderful stress relievers. When we're upset or uncertain, talking while feeling heard is the best gift we can get. It settles our feelings and reassures us of our value as a person. Doing crafts, creating art, playing music, and gardening are time-honored ways to release stress. Focusing on the stitch or the note or the weeds has a way of calmly directing our attention and soothing our thoughts. Sometimes just a hug or a little cuddle time can help both her and us feel so much better.

It's important to remember that stress isn't all bad, either. Some stress can be a positive part of life. It can motivate us to make a change or take a risk that's good for us. It can improve our performance and add an extra jolt of energy, if we're not overwhelmed by it. So don't try to make your daughter's life stress free. Not only would it be boring, but it's impossible!

What to Say and Do

1–7 YEARS OLD
Help her pace herself, recognizing when she needs a break.

- It's been a long wait. I think we could both use a little cuddle time right now.

- You look a little tense. Want to come outside and play fetch with the dog?

Teach her how to read her own stress signs.

- Your face looks kind of tight. Are you feeling stressed?

- You aren't very hungry tonight. Are you feeling uptight?

Ask about her feelings when she seems stressed.

- How are you feeling right now?

8–13 YEARS OLD
Help her learn what relaxes her body: running, yoga, walking, or a back rub.

- When does your body feel relaxed?

- Let's shoot some hoops and loosen up before dinner.

Share activities that relieve stress for you and see if they calm her.

- Gardening really relaxes me. How about you?

- Would a back rub feel good?

■ When I'm really stressed, I feel much better after a warm shower.

Help her accept that stress is a normal part of life and that she can manage it.

■ We all feel stressed sometimes.

■ You handle your stress very creatively.

■ You felt so tense but you're calm now that we talked.

14 AND UP
Explain that stress can signal a problem she needs to solve.

■ When a little thing really bothers me, it usually means there's a bigger issue underneath it that I need to do something about.

■ Could your tension about the test mean that you feel you could have studied better?

■ It seems like something else is behind that annoyance. What do you think?

What Not to Say and Do

Don't dismiss her feelings of stress. Don't say,

■ What are you complaining about?

■ You don't have stress.

■ Stop whining about it.

Don't encourage her to cope with stress by consumption: eating, drinking, or shopping. Don't say,

■ You're upset. How about a bowl of ice cream?

■ I thought this new sweater would cheer you up.

Words and Phrases to Avoid

- Life's just a pain.

- Get used to it.

- Don't stress.

Resources

Dealing with the Stuff That Makes Life Tough: The 10 Things That Stress Girls Out and How to Cope with Them by Jill Zimmerman Rutledge. McGraw-Hill, 2003.

Everything You Need to Know about Stress by Eleanor H. Ayer. Rosen Publishing, 2001.

Fighting Invisible Tigers: A Stress Management Guide for Teens by Earl Hipp. Free Spirit Publishing, 1996.

Stress Relief: The Ultimate Teen Guide (It Happened to Me, 3) by Mark Powell, illustrated by Kelly Adams Rowman & Littlefield, 2002.

TELEPHONES AND PAGERS

"If I let her, Angelina would talk on the phone with her friends from the minute she got home from school until she went to bed. She'd probably fall asleep talking if I let her stay on the phone! She spends the whole day with those girls. Why does she need to be on the phone with them all night?"—Juan

Things to Consider

Connections and relationships with friends are very important to girls' development. Our daughters define themselves and explore who they are through relationships. When younger, they do this primarily through the family. Around the middle school years, this development shifts to a girl's friendships. She wants to stay in touch with friends because it's important to her sense of self. In healthy friendships, talking with a friend helps her process feelings and make good decisions. And the telephone is a great way to stay in touch, no matter where she and her friends are.

It's a good idea to set time limits for phone calls and rules about how the family shares the phone. Keep an open mind about what her time on the phone is all about. She may just as likely be talking about homework or play practice as gossip. In middle school, keep an ear out for what the conversation generally seems to be about, and ask questions if you suspect phone calls are being used to maintain cliques or manipulate your daughter or others. If that's happening, don't let it continue.

By the time she's in high school, it's important to respect the privacy of her calls. If you have serious concerns about things like drug or alcohol use, you need to address those without eavesdropping on her calls. You may want to give her a cell phone so she can always reach you and you can reach her.

What to Say and Do

8 AND UP
Create clear rules about length and frequency of calls and use of pagers.

- You can talk on the phone either before dinner or after your homework is done.

- When I need to use the phone, I'll let you know and you need to finish up in five minutes.

- No answering the phone during meals.

Listen to her proposals about phone and pager rules and fairly evaluate them.

- You think the ten-minute limit per call is too strict. What do you think would be reasonable?

- How will you balance doing your homework and staying in touch with your friends?

If you want to know what she was talking about, ask her.

- It sounded like you were upset during that call. What was going on?

Words and Phrases to Use

- Limits
- Guidelines
- Balance
- Respect
- Share phone time.

- Do you want privacy for this call?
- Connection
- Communication
- In touch

What Not to Say and Do

Don't yell at her to get off the phone. Don't say,

- Hang up right now!
- I told you not to talk so long. Get off that phone!

Don't listen in on her phone calls secretly.

Don't be overly restrictive of her phone use unless you've tried to handle it with discussion and that hasn't worked.

Don't tease her when she's on the phone.

TOMBOYS

"Elyse already gets teased by other girls because she doesn't dress girly or like to play girls' games. She seems to feel more comfortable being friends with boys. And she loves to play hockey and is the only girl on her team. How will she adjust when she gets to puberty? I don't want her to feel like a misfit."
—Jackie

Things to Consider

Girls have more freedom than boys do to explore both traditional male and female gender roles while young. People often accept girls acting boyish until they are in the middle elementary grades. At that point, other kids and adults can get very uncomfortable with a girl who still seems to prefer "boy" activities. She may get both subtle and overt suggestions that she's not acting like a real girl and that there's something strange about her. People may unconsciously feel that being a tomboy for "too long" means she is homosexual. That may or may not be the case, but the ostracism she could receive in that situation is very painful and confusing to her and us.

As parents, we want to encourage our daughters in being true to themselves. But it gets difficult for us to do that if being true to herself means being different than the culture expects her to be. In addition to wanting her to feel comfortable with herself, we want her to be accepted by society. It's hard to cope if our daughter doesn't "fit in" and we feel a conflict about what's really in her best interest. Having a daughter who's a tomboy may be the earliest way we face this dilemma with our girls. Fortunately, our culture is getting more accepting of people who blend female and male behaviors according to their own recipe. In the end, supporting her in being her true self and helping her find the friends and situations where she feels that she fits in are the best things we can do.

What to Say and Do

1–7 YEARS OLD
Accept her likes and dislikes in friends, activities, and clothing. They're coming from her heart.

- You like to wear pants more than dresses. So do I.
- Josh is a good friend to you.

8–13 YEARS OLD
Help her stay true to herself when she gets pressure to fit the girl stereotype. Tell her girls can be all different ways, not just a few ways.

- Some girls like to play hockey and some don't. That's OK.
- You can do karate and ballet both if you want.

If she feels excluded by other girls, help her decide how to handle that and find groups and activities where she has things in common with other kids.

- It sounds like Pearl is friendly to you even when the popular girls aren't.
- Even if you tried to change yourself, they might not be any nicer.
- People who want you to act just like them aren't true friends.

14 AND UP
Let her play around with her identity when she feels the need. Show her you know she's still herself no matter how she changes her appearance.

- Today it looks like you're showing your girlish side with that makeup and hairdo.

- Your short haircut is fun and playful, like you feel more free.

- When you wear that flannel shirt, you look really comfortable.

Words and Phrases to Use

- Your self
- What do you like?
- What's fun for you?
- What feels right for you?

- What do you want?
- I like you.
- You're my girl.

What Not to Say and Do

Don't tell her she's not acting like a girl. The way she acts doesn't determine whether or not she's a girl. Don't say,

- Girls don't do that.

- What's the matter with you?

- Only boys like to play tackle football.

Don't give her the message she has to change herself for other's expectations. Don't say,

- The girls won't like you if you dress like that.

- People might think you're gay.

- Gramma will be upset if you wear your hair like a boy.

Don't make negative remarks about women or men who are outside our culture's gender stereotypes.

Words and Phrases to Avoid

- You should change.
- It's lonely to be different.
- Why are you like that?
- Where did we go wrong?

- No one will like you.
- You're strange.
- Peculiar

TRADITIONS

"My fifteen-year-old Hanna has all of a sudden gotten really interested in our family history. She's wanting to know about my great-grandparents and grilling me for details about how we did Thanksgiving and Yom Kippur when I was a kid. It's great, but where is this sudden burst coming from?"—Roger

Things to Consider

Many of us don't live near our extended families anymore, making it harder to stay connected to them and harder to easily build a natural community of family and neighbors. The instinct for family and community is powerful in humans, and it's reinforced in girls by the cultural expectation that females are supposed to keep family relationships strong.

Family stories and traditions are interesting and comforting, and can be powerful tools for building a strong self-worth in girls. For example, regular visits to Grandma's photo album help girls resist the pressure of conforming to cultural beauty myths by showing how our physical features are primarily genetic and immutable. Coupling knowledge that "Stein women have always had prominent chins and kinky black hair" with stories about ancestral accomplishments and quirks can help a girl feel proud, even if she doesn't fit today's narrow definition of "beauty" (which very few people do). Those fun stories and pictures also help us adults feel good about our own heritage.

Plus, our heritage is a rich source of family rituals, which also tend to be scarce in our mobile, frenetic culture. For years, researchers have found that kids have fewer problems the more often they sit down to dinner with their families (and without a TV) and spend holidays together.

What to Say and Do

1–7 YEARS OLD

Girls this age love the excitement and rituals of holidays. Integrate your favorite traditions from your families (and/or friends) with ideas your kids create. Keep doing them year to year, especially the ones the kids enjoy most.

- I'm using your great-grandma's recipe this year. Do you want to learn it with me?

- Let's start collecting ornaments that only you get to put on the tree each year and then take with you when you grow up.

- Call Grandpa and ask him to show us his family slides when we visit him this summer.

8–13 YEARS OLD

Girls this age can start tracing the history of their own life and immediate family. Make it a fun process and not like a school project.

- Let's write a story or draw some pictures about your first memories as a little girl.

- Here are my baby pictures. Did you ever hear the story about where my parents were living and what they were doing when I was little?

- I am so proud of the way you are strong and smart. You remind me of your great-aunt who was widowed young but went on to become a police officer back when few women did that.

14 AND UP

As girls start to see friends with complex, blended families (or start to live in one themselves), they may seek comfort in the continuity of their family heritage and tradition. Use this as a helpful tool.

■ Let's get copies of Grandma's photos and combine them with ours so we can make an album tracing as far back in the family as we can.

■ You're old enough now, and I'd like you to say the family prayer (or make the family toast) before Thanksgiving dinner this year.

■ Which of your relatives do you aspire to be like? Tell me why.

Actions to Use

■ Honor the traditions that give your daughter pleasure, even if they seem silly to you.

■ Regularly use family history as a tool to boost her self-esteem.

■ Tell both the funny and inspiring stories about your ancestors; after all, it's important not to take yourself too seriously.

What Not to Say and Do

Don't belittle or ridicule traditions your children create or ridicule the heritage and rituals of your child's other relatives. Don't say,

■ That's a stupid idea.

■ Do we really have to do something that's so much trouble?

■ Boy, was your great-grandfather ever ugly!

■ We don't have time for holiday traditions.

Words and Phrases to Avoid

- I can't be expected to be home for dinner; I have too much work to do.

- All that religious holiday stuff is a bunch of mumbo jumbo.

- Your mother's family is a bunch of jerks, and I don't give them the time of day.

Resources

The Book of New Family Traditions: How to Create Great Rituals for Holidays and Everyday by Meg Cox. Running Press, 2003.

Family Traditions: 289 Things to Do Again and Again by Caryl Waller Krueger. Belleridge Press, 1998.

TV AND POPULAR CULTURE

"Javan seems to be overly influenced by the stuff she sees in magazines and on TV. Her tastes are set by ads she's seen, and she talks about celebrities like they were real friends and role models. The music she listens to is incomprehensible to me, and I think it gives bad messages about women. I don't seem to be able to break in."—John

Things to Consider

Our daughters live in a pop culture created by media, not by reality. Do yourself and your daughter the favor of reading current research and opinions about TV, video games, magazines, music, and movies so you can decide how you want to handle them. The average girl spends forty-one times as much time watching television as she does in substantive conversations with her parents. Add on time in front of a computer or teen magazines, and the ratio gets even more out of whack. Popular culture has a huge effect on every girl, even those who don't consume nearly as much popular media as the average. We can't make TV or pop culture disappear, so we have two major challenges.

First, we need to understand that media is a language that we and our children must be literate in. Media's vocabulary is made up of words and images (the images are usually more powerful and prominent). Media's grammar is how the words and images (vocabulary) are put together to communicate meaning and motivate the consumer to act. Second, we need to make concerted, conscious efforts to look at our own use of media and substitute family time for media time in our homes and our lives. If left to their own devices, our children can easily adopt the media's values and accept the pop culture as the only culture.

What to Say and Do

1–7 YEARS OLD

Decide on a weekly "minutes budget" of electronic media and stick with it. Some experts recommend no electronic media at all before age three because it's so passive.

Young children don't have the developmental capacity to tell make-believe from reality, especially in visually saturated media like TV. Talk to her about the level of unreality in media, and dedicate a lot of time to developing her imagination *without* electronic media.

- Let's go outside and play!

- Look at the pictures in this magazine. Do you know people who look like that?

- TV and movies aren't real. People spend a lot of time and money to make them look perfect. I think real life, like at our house, is more interesting most days.

Ask extended family, child-care providers, and close friends to respect your media limits when your child visits them unless you agree to a different plan.

- We think it's healthy to limit how much she watches TV and movies and plays video games. Thanks for helping.

- We'd rather have her playing outside or reading than watching TV or movies.

When she consumes electronic media, have an adult with her to provide conversation, commentary, and context for what she sees.

- It seems like all the girls in this movie act pretty ridiculous. How do you feel about it?

- I don't like it when the girl needs to be rescued all the time. What do you think?

8–13 YEARS OLD

Don't put a TV or video game machine in her bedroom. Keep them in a public part of the house so she's not isolated when using them.

Set a new weekly "electronic-media budget" based on the limits you feel will be best for her. Listen to her feelings but still decide on the rules yourself. If she's ready for it, let her start to set some of her own limits as she gets older.

- No TV, video games, or movies on school nights.

- You can have one hour of TV, movies, or video games if all your homework is done before dinner.

Keep the hour before bedtime free of electronic media. It will help her relax and sleep better.

Provide many alternatives for ways to relax and enjoy herself like art materials, board games, puzzles, noncompetitive sports, theater, books, good magazines, chess, instruments, and crafts. Do them with her sometimes.

In pre- and early adolescence, media saturation tends to reinforce negative peer pressure and self-image among girls. Keep the conversation and education around media going.

- Let's look closely at this magazine cover. Guess what you have that she doesn't: Pores! Yes, the model does have pores, but that's one of the things they erase in photo sessions. That's not how she looks in real life.

- What things do you think girls are doing just because TV or pop culture says it's cool? What do you think of that?

Help her literally deconstruct media by cutting up old magazines to create her own alternative ads.

- In this teen magazine, which ad or article do you think is the worst. Why?

- Let's get out scissors and glue and make an "anti-ad" to respond to this one.

- What ad or article do you find inspiring? Why?

- Let's listen to that CD together. I'd love to hear what you like best about it.

- Make alternative magazines and movies available at home all the time.

14 AND UP

Put her in charge of her own electronic-media budget as long as she doesn't have an addictive reliance on it. Allow real-world consequences to happen.

- This year you can propose your own electronic media budget, and we'll negotiate it with you.

- I know it's hard for you to get up this morning after being up till 1 a.m. watching that movie, but you still have to get up.

Encourage your girl to state bold opinions about the media she sees. Encourage her to critique it, and especially to compare it to the reality of her own life.

- I'm surprised to hear you say that. Tell me more about your thinking.

- How do the situations in that movie compare to our life here? Here are the pros and cons of each as I see it. What do you think?

Help her identify contradictions and harmful stereotypes about media portrayals of body image, stereotypes, violence, and other issues affecting her.

- Does anyone in the circle of people you know really look like that actress? I bet she doesn't even look like that.

- Do you think kids in your school are as obsessed with violence as it seems like they are on TV?

- Are all blondes dumb?

Read the print media that she consumes (magazines, comic books, and so on) and comment to her about it. Strengthen your own family with time and real stories shared together.

Words and Phrases to Use

- Media budget

- Choose

- Options

- Limits

- Expectations

What Not to Say and Do

Don't use electronic media as a reward or withhold it as a punishment so it takes on a sense of forbidden fruit.

- If you're good in the grocery store, you can watch TV when we get home.

- As long as you keep a B average, you can have a TV in your room.

Don't be hypocritical by limiting her electronic media more than you're willing to limit your own use of it.

Don't refuse to watch shows she's interested in.

- That's kid stuff. I'm not going to watch with you.

- That's a waste of time; I'm too busy to watch it with you.

Censorship often creates the "forbidden fruit" attraction in children. Don't,

- Ban specific things unless you have looked at them and discussed them with her.

- Stop telling her what you think about media even if she doesn't always like what you say.

- Dismiss her media choices out of hand, without listening to (and taking seriously) her reasons for wanting that media.

It's easy to let media take over as "the other parent" after a long day. Don't,

- Let media be a babysitter.

- Tune in the TV more than you tune in your daughter.

- Accept her unthinking usage of hurtful or disrespectful interactions she sees on TV shows.

- Say, "I don't have time to see that movie before you do. Go ahead and go; it'll be all right."

Words and Phrases to Avoid

- If you're good, I'll get you that video game.

- Don't get upset. It's just a movie.

Resources

Can't Buy My Love: How Advertising Changes the Way We Think and Feel by Jean Kilbourne. Simon & Schuster, 2000. (more information at www.jeankilbourne.com)

Four Arguments for the Elimination of Television by Jerry Mander. William Morrow, 1978.

"Mommy, I'm Scared": How TV and Movies Frighten Children and What We Can Do to Protect Them by Joanne Cantor. Harcourt, 1998.

The Other Parent: The Inside Story of the Media's Effect on Our Children by Jim Steyer. Atria, 2002.

The Plug-In Drug: Television, Computers and Family Life by Marie Winn. Penguin, 2002.

Adbusters: www.adbusters.org

Dads and Daughters: www.dadsanddaughters.org

See Jane: www.seejane.org

Just Think: www.justthink.org

Mind on the Media: www.tbio.org

National Institute on Media and the Family: www.mediafamily.org

Center for Media Education, 1511 K Street, NW, Suite 518, Washington, DC 20005. Phone: (202) 628-2620. www.cme.org

Common Sense Media: www.commonsensemedia.org

TV Turnoff: www.tvturnoff.org

VEGETARIANISM

"Aliyah has suddenly decided she wants to be a vegetarian because she feels that killing animals is wrong. Only for her that seems to mean eating only bread, French fries, juice, and desserts. I know she's not getting a balanced diet. I have to do something about what she's eating, but I don't want to turn this into a battle of wills like food was between me and my mom."—Fatima

Things to Consider

Many preteen and teen girls experiment with vegetarianism. And it can be a healthy choice, contrary to what many parents think. You may be surprised to learn the benefits of not eating meat. First, educate yourself about vegetarianism and what makes for a healthy vegetarian diet. Then, your response needs to take into account the reason your daughter is interested in vegetarianism.

Many girls are motivated by their love of animals. If she's concerned about animal welfare, then she'll have some motivation to learn about healthy vegetarian food balance and try various foods. You can share what you've learned and give her some shared responsibility for preparing special vegetarian dishes. Many more try it because it's popular. If she's trying it only because it's popular, she'll probably be less committed and will respond best to your firm insistence that she balance her foods on a daily basis. And some girls try it as a way to control their diet and have an acceptable excuse for restricting what they eat. If you suspect that she has the warning signs of an eating disorder and her interest in vegetarianism might be a way to restrict food, you need to get professional help, starting with calling her doctor. In this situation, the health benefits of vegetarianism are moot and don't factor into the equation at all.

What to Say and Do

8 AND UP

Figure out why she's interested in vegetarianism, listening to what she says and how she acts.

- Tell me how you got interested in vegetarianism.

- I'm sure there's a Web site or a cookbook where we can get more information about how to do it right.

- I respect your concern about animals and not wanting them killed. Vegetarian eating can be healthy and delicious.

If she's serious enough to eat healthy and vegetarian, help her do that responsibly, meeting her halfway.

- We're having pasta tonight so I made some of the sauce without meat for you.

- Let's find some yummy recipes that the whole family can try because we can't make two totally different meals every night.

- I wonder what combines with peanut butter to make a complete protein?

- If you don't want to eat the turkey, what could you have instead?

As she gets older, give her responsibility for preparing dinner once or twice a week, and she can make vegetarian dishes on her nights.

Keep the focus on eating for health and nutrition, whether vegetarian or not.

Pay attention to how healthy you eat as parents. It's unreasonable to expect your daughter to be a healthier eater than you are.

Words and Phrases to Use

- Health
- Nutrition
- Balance

- Energy
- Delicious
- Family meals

What Not to Say and Do

Don't make it into a battle by refusing to learn about vegetarianism or meet her halfway. Don't say,

- I can't cook without meat. It's the only thing Dad likes.
- This is all there is for dinner. Eat it or go hungry.
- Tofu is weird and disgusting.

Words and Phrases to Avoid

- That's crazy!
- They're just animals.
- You hate vegetables.
- It's just a fad.

VIOLENCE

"I was shocked when Shiraz came home from school today and told me that two girls in her class were suspended for fighting. I know that girls hurt each other emotionally, but since when did they start actually hitting each other? We've always told her to work out conflicts with words, but now I'm worried that she'll be vulnerable if girls are being physically violent. What can I say to her?"—Jonelle

Things to Consider

Violence is terrifying to parents. Our strongest desire is to keep our children safe, no matter what. Our worst nightmare is that our daughters might be physically harmed, and we work hard to protect them from that possibility. At the same time, we don't want them to be physically violent and hurt anyone else. The combination of our fears and feelings can make this a difficult issue for parents to find balance on.

Starting at a young age, we teach our daughters not to hit or kick when they're angry, even when someone else hits them. At the same time, we teach them skills to protect them from potentially violent adults. As they get older, we want to be sure that they won't accept violence from a boyfriend and will realize it's a sign of a bad relationship. The interaction between violence and self-defense is complicated for her to negotiate. The best course is to talk openly and explore both her feelings and your concerns as you help her learn to live in our imperfect world.

What to Say and Do

1–7 YEARS OLD

Teach her ways to express anger strongly without physical violence.

- ■ You're really angry and you can scream really, really loud until it's all out.

Teach her that no one should ever hit, kick, physically threaten, or bite her and that she can peacefully confront violence with your support.

- ■ Bobby was really angry, but it wasn't OK for him to push you. We'll talk to him and the teacher about it tomorrow.

8–13 YEARS OLD

Continue to emphasize and show her ways to resolve her frustrations and arguments without violence.

- ■ I was so frustrated I felt like kicking someone, but instead I went outside and kicked the soccer ball really hard until I felt calmer.

Role-play situations with her so she develops confidence in how she could respond if someone threatens violence.

- ■ What could you do if someone told you you had to fight her to defend yourself?

Take a self-defense or martial arts class with her. You'll both feel more confidence in your strength and physical security and will rehearse scenarios that build your defense skills.

Matter-of-factly discuss how to logically assess situations and steer clear of possibly unsafe ones.

14 AND UP

When she starts dating, teach her about the warning signs of controlling behavior by a boyfriend or girlfriend that can precede violence. If you observe or hear about any violent behavior, take action immediately to end the relationship and get help for the perpetrator.

- It's disrespectful for Jake to make you feel guilty about spending time with your friends.

- I'm very upset to hear that Marcus joked about punching Tom. We need to talk about this.

Emotional violence, like shaming, manipulating, and belittling, can also be a problem in dating relationships and be a warning of potential physical violence.

Words and Phrases to Use

- Safety
- Strength
- Confidence
- Practice
- Self-defense
- Techniques
- Peace

- Security
- Calm
- Get help.
- Tell me.
- Nonviolence
- Mutual respect

What Not to Say and Do

Don't make her fearful to try to protect her from violence. Don't say,

- You can't go anywhere after dark, no matter what.
- You better stay home.
- You never know what they might do.

Don't ever suggest violence as a solution or as something to be tolerated and ignored.

- Sometimes you have to fight to prove your point.
- He just pushed you; just forget it.

Words and Phrases to Avoid

- Victim
- Helpless
- Forget about it.
- That didn't really hurt.
- Boys will be boys.

Resources

Saving Beauty from the Beast: How to Protect Your Daughter from an Unhealthy Relationship by Vicki Crompton. Little, Brown, 2003.

VOLUNTEERISM

"We want to encourage our kids to contribute to the community, and so we're starting to require them to join us in various volunteer activities. They're dragging their feet, saying none of their friends do this. Will making them volunteer backfire and discourage them from doing it in the future?"—Steve

Things to Consider

Volunteering is a wonderful thing for families and for kids. It can be especially good during the teen years when they are naturally self-centered! For girls in particular, volunteering gives them a chance to learn new skills and be recognized for their compassion, work, and contributions rather than their appearance or popularity. It creates a place where they belong separate from school and friendships, and that can give girls a balancing perspective on themselves. It can also be a way to explore possible careers they might fantasize about.

If your daughter isn't excited about volunteering when you first bring it up, do it anyway. Don't make it a punishment, but be clear that the whole family is going to do this and that it's not negotiable. Do ask her if she prefers a certain volunteer activity to another, and listen to her preference. She may not act enthusiastic, but if you let her express those feelings and still carry through, the experience will give her its own rewards. An added bonus is that kids who volunteer often get a lot of positive feedback from adults, and every girl can use that boost. Last but not least, giving of her energy and skills to others feels great!

What to Say and Do

1–7 YEARS OLD
When practical, bring her along when you volunteer and let her play while you work.

At these ages a physical activity (like the food shelf) is best suited for her to actually help.

8–13 YEARS OLD
Make volunteering a regular family activity. Get her input on what she'd like to volunteer for and support that.

- The antiviolence walk is next month, and we're all going to get pledges and walk together.

- You can choose our family volunteer project for next month. What would you like to do?

She may start volunteering on her own or with friends as she gets older. That's great, but keep some volunteering as a family activity. She can invite a friend if she likes, but the focus is still on the family doing it together.

- It's great that you do the trail maintenance with your scout troop. We're still going to do Habitat for Humanity as a family.

- Would you like to invite Celina to come with us?

Emphasize the dignity of the people her volunteering is helping and that we all need help at one time or another.

14 AND UP
She may choose some volunteer activities that you're not as comfortable with. As long as it's a legitimate group with reasonable safety precautions, support her heartfelt choices.

- You feel strongly about fighting antigay bias, and I support you working on it.

■ What does the group do so people don't take their angry feelings out on the volunteers during the rally?

Words and Phrases to Use

■ Giving

■ Generous

■ Helping

■ Compassion

■ Activism

■ Community

■ Fun

■ Rewarding

■ Responsible

■ Talents

■ Teamwork

■ Supportive

What Not to Say and Do

Don't make volunteering a punishment for bad behavior.

Don't be unrealistic in how much volunteering you expect. Five hours a month is a good start.

Don't discount volunteering she does outside organized groups (like picking up litter as she walks down the street).

Resources

The Busy Family's Guide to Volunteering: Doing Good Together by Jenny Friedman. Gryphon House, 2003.

Get Involved! A Girl's Guide to Volunteering by Erin M. Hovanec. Rosen Publishing, 1999.

Teens with the Courage to Give: Young People Who Triumphed over Tragedy and Volunteered to Make a Difference by Jackie Waldman. Red Wheel/Weiser, 2000.

WOMEN'S HISTORY AND ROLE MODELS

"There are so many interesting women in history, but hardly any of them are in my daughter's textbooks. How do I get her interested in this when she thinks history is boring?"—Matsu

Things to Consider

Knowing the richness of women's history can make girls feel proud and stretch their ideas of what they may do one day. It connects them to the long line of women and girls who came before them and made the world a better place, inspiring them to do the same. Women in history are role models that teach girls and boys about valuable personal qualities and how to overcome problems. We all deserve a full picture of history that we can relate to.

What to Say and Do

1–7 YEARS OLD
Give her many books and videos about women and girls in history.
Help her see how she's making her own history every day.

■ Here are pictures of your first overnight at Grandad's on your own. You were brave.

■ Remember when you and Jacqui learned to ride your bikes and how many times you fell off?

8 AND UP
Take her to visit women's history sites.

■ This is where the tea party was that started the movement for women to get the vote.

■ This house was a stop on the Underground Railroad where two sisters hid escaping slaves.

Talk with her teachers about what's missing in her textbooks and why women's history is important.

■ Here's a great Web site for lots of women's biographies.

■ I'm concerned that the students are only getting part of the picture of history.

Talk about women's achievements and how they've been minimized in traditional history.

Talk about women alive today who are making history around the world.

Help her see women from history as real people with weaknesses as well as strengths.

Words and Phrases to Use

■ Achievement

■ Overcoming inequality

■ Pioneering

■ Living by their beliefs

■ Bravery

■ Risk taking

■ Leadership

What Not to Say and Do

Don't leave her knowledge of history to what she gets in textbooks. It's too limited.

Don't buy into the view that women haven't been important in history just because they're not in the textbooks.

Words and Phrases to Avoid

- History is all about dead men.
- History is boring.
- History is all dates and battles.

Resources

A Is for Abigail: An Almanac of Amazing American Women by Lynne Cheney. Simon & Schuster, 2003.

American Girl historical novels published by Pleasant Company Publications.

Founding Mothers: The Women Who Raised Our Nation by Cokie Roberts. Harper-Collins, 2004.

Susan B. Anthony Slept Here: A Guide to American Women's Landmarks by Jurate Kazickas and Lynn Sherr. Time Books, 1994.

National Women's History Project: www.nwhp.org

New Moon Magazine Herstory articles: www.newmoon.org

WOMEN'S RIGHTS

"I want my daughter Anne to learn about women's rights and feel proud of being female. She takes equal rights for granted, and I don't think she understands how much hard work went into getting the changes to happen. And of course there are still things that aren't equal."—Irene

Things to Consider

The women's movement of the last century dramatically improved women's and girls' self-determination, opportunities, and lives. There is still work to be done, just as there is in civil rights and other justice movements. When she's younger, you can help her understand what equal rights are in the particulars of her daily life. As she gets older, discuss things that are unequal and help her see how she can join with others to change them.

Preadolescent girls can be acutely aware of injustice (how many times have you heard, "That's not fair!"), and parents may discount some of this as just complaining. Take the time to think about whether it's just whining or if the thing she's complaining about is a larger issue that deserves work. If it is, be her ally in working to right a wrong for girls and women.

What to Say and Do

8–13 YEARS OLD

Give her books to read that help her understand and relate to women's and girls' lives when they had fewer rights.

- Can you believe that women couldn't even have their own bank account?

- Imagine what it would be like to be twelve and have to marry someone you'd never met.

Take her concerns about injustice seriously, and listen carefully when she talks about them. Help her decide if she wants to take action.

- It sounds like your science teacher has outdated ideas about girls. Do you want to do anything about it?

- You're right; it's not fair that the girls' teams have to hold car washes to buy uniforms but the football team doesn't.

14 AND UP

Introduce her to the ways that groups work successfully against injustice.

- To get the vote, women's groups worked for a long time and tried a lot of different things.

- When women decided being paid less for the same work was unfair, they went to court to fight for their rights.

Emphasize the rewards of supporting a cause you believe in even if you don't win every battle along the way.

Words and Phrases to Use

- Equality
- Fairness
- Collaboration
- Action
- Protests
- Politics

- Improvement
- Hope
- Justice
- Human rights
- The power of people

What Not to Say and Do

Don't give her the impression that she can't do anything about injustice. Don't say,

- It's always been that way and it always will.
- People tried to change that already and it didn't work.
- You just have to accept it. People will never change.

Words and Phrases to Avoid

- All or nothing—if it's not all equal, then nothing's equal.
- Hopelessness
- Inaction
- Apathy

Resources

33 Things Every Girl Should Know about Women's History, edited by Tanya Bolden. Crown Publishing, 2002.

America's Women: Four Hundred Years of Dolls, Drudges, Helpmates, and Heroines by Gail Collins. HarperCollins, 2003.

WORK AND CAREERS

"How can I help my daughter have an open mind about all the different things she might do for work when she's grown up?"—Cheryl

Things to Consider

Any kind of work or career is open to women today, but there are still many well-paying fields where women are underrepresented, including science, technology, building trades, and business upper management. On average, women earn significantly less than men during their lifetimes and have lower retirement savings as a result, even though they live longer than men.

When she's old enough to work for pay, try to help her find opportunities that expand her horizons like doing lawn work or pet sitting in addition to babysitting. If she wants a part-time job when she's sixteen, be sure to limit the work hours so it doesn't interfere with school. As adults, our daughters will face the challenge of balancing paid work and family, if they decide to have children or are involved in caring for us when we get older. Ironically, all the choices can feel overwhelming to a girl. She will benefit from your help in exploring work that uses her talents and pays well enough to support her financially.

What to Say and Do

1–7 YEARS OLD

Encourage her imaginative play to include all kinds of future careers, especially those where women are underrepresented.

- Let's pretend we're pioneers going to live on the moon. You're the captain of the spaceship.

8–13 YEARS OLD

Bring her to work with you and ask others to let her visit their workplaces, too. Direct experience is important to help girls imagine themselves doing something.

- Aunt Julie is going to take you to work in the lab with her for a day during spring vacation.
- Jon said you can ride in the bulldozer with him when he's working on our driveway.

Help her find volunteer opportunities that let her experience various kinds of work.

- We can ask the vet if you can come in and help out on Saturday mornings.
- My club needs a new web page. Can you help me learn how to create it?

14 AND UP

Show her how you balance work and family. Share household responsibilities fairly between all the adults.

- Your stepdad enjoys baking more than I do, so he does most of it.

Emphasize and applaud her pride and responsibility in work.

- The manager knows she can count on you to do your best.
- You did that so efficiently. I'm impressed with what you've learned at work.

Even uninteresting jobs at this age can be valuable because they may motivate her to go on to college so she can get more challenging work.

- I know that job is boring for you. You want to earn the money, so you're making the best of it for the summer.

Words and Phrases to Use

- Choice
- Fulfillment
- Responsibility
- Earning

- Dependability
- Fair pay
- Fair share

What Not to Say and Do

Don't give her the message that a career is out of reach because she's a girl. Don't say,

- Leave that technical stuff to the guys.
- The odds aren't good for women in that field. I just don't want you to be disappointed.
- I wanted to be a truck driver, but women aren't strong enough for that.

Don't imply that she'll be locked into any career she talks about. Don't say,

- Are you sure you'll want to be doing that in twenty years?
- If you want to have kids, you'll have to just focus on them and take any job you can get.

Words, Phrases, and Actions to Avoid

- That's just a fantasy.

- We'll never be able to afford for you to go to medical school.

- It doesn't matter what it pays.

- Grumbling about your job without taking constructive action to change it.

Resources

Cool Careers for Girls by Ceel Pasternak and Linda Thornburg (series about many different careers). Impact Publishing.

I Could Do Anything If I Only Knew What It Was: How to Discover What You Really Want and How to Get It by Barbara Sher and Barbara Smith. Dell, 1995.

What Color Is Your Parachute? 2004: A Practical Guide for Job-Hunters and Career-Changers by Richard Nelson Bolles. Ten Speed Press, 2004.

Young Women of Achievement: A Resource for Girls in Science, Math, and Technology by Frances A. Karnes. Prometheus, 2002.

Take Our Daughters and Sons to Work Day: www.todstw.org

New Moon Magazine Women's articles: www.newmoon.org

WORRIES

"My daughter is eleven and going through a really tough time lately with worrying about everything. She worries that she might get sick, that she may die, or that others will die and worries about getting homesick when she is away. You name it, she worries about it. Do you have any advice on how to cope with these feelings?" —Janetta

Things to Consider

Sometimes fears signal real danger, but often they are out of proportion to the real threat. You want to teach your daughter how to recognize her fears, assess their relationship to real dangers, and cope with them accordingly. At times she will need your help with fears, and other times she can handle them on her own. Feeling that she can talk with you about her fears at any time is important, even if they are fears she can handle herself. When her worries are based in a real danger, do what you can to keep her protected from the danger so she feels as safe as she can. If you can't protect her, help her process her feelings of fear so they don't disable her.

Distinguishing between the fears she can handle and the ones she needs help with is important to her emotional well-being. Being able to do this makes her feel capable, strong, and supported. However, if fears and worries start to take over your daughter's thoughts and affect her peace of mind, you will need to do more than just listen and reassure her. If worries are keeping her from doing things she wants to do, you may need to get professional help for her.

What to Say and Do

1–7 YEARS OLD
Listen to her fears openly and accept them. Give her both verbal and physical reassurance that her feelings are normal.

- It sounds like you feel scared.

- Let me give you a hug.

After she's expressed her worry, stay calm and help her figure out what she can do to cope with it.

- Will it help to leave the light on in your closet?

- Those waves are big; I can hold your hand while you get used to them.

8–13 YEARS OLD
If her worries start to focus on one particular thing, look for experiences that may have triggered them.

- You've been worried about your homework since you got a D on that project.

- I've noticed that you're feeling worried since I talked about the layoffs at my job.

If you can't find a direct cause, obsessive worrying may be the way she is expressing some other anxiety that she's not consciously aware of. Make calm observations and ask open-ended questions.

- You're worried about us all getting sick, but I think there might be something else behind that.

- Worrying has kept you from going on sleepovers lately. What do you think that's about?

14 AND UP

Own and express your fears and worries openly. Let her see you accepting and coping with your own fears in a positive way, including asking for support and help when needed.

- I'm taking a workshop so I can deal with my fear of public speaking and work for a promotion.

- Can you give me a hug? I'm worried about Grammy having cancer. It's scary since I can't do anything about it.

She'll naturally cope with her worries more and more on her own as she gets older. Stay tuned in to what she's feeling and offer listening and emotional support so she can deal with her fears.

Words and Phrases to Use

- Safe

- Secure

- I'm here.

- I'll help you.

- Support

- It's OK to be afraid.

- You can do it even if you're worried.

What Not to Say and Do

Don't tell her to ignore her fears—that will just drive them underground. Don't say,

- That's nothing to worry about.

- I'm tired of hearing about your worries. Nothing's that big a deal when you're a kid.

Don't be a worrywart yourself. Don't say,

- ■ You can't do that because it worries me.

Words and Phrases to Avoid

- ■ It's silly to be afraid of that.

- ■ That's not even real.

- ■ You're a sissy.

- ■ Don't worry.

Resources

Monsters under the Bed and Other Childhood Fears: Helping Your Child Overcome Anxieties, Fears, and Phobias by Stephen W. Garber. Random House, 1993.

The Scared Child: Helping Kids Overcome Traumatic Events by Barbara A. Brooks and Paula M. Siegel. John Wiley & Sons, 1996.

Up and Down the Worry Hill: A Children's Book about Obsessive-Compulsive Disorder and Its Treatment by Aureen Pinto Wagner, illustrated by Paul A. Jutton. Lighthouse Press, 2000.

Wemberly Worried by Kevin Henkes. Greenwillow Books, 2000.

RESOURCES

Daughters: For Parents of Girls: www.daughters.com (a bimonthly newsletter with practical tips for parents of girls ages eight to sixteen. Individual articles on many topics can be purchased on the Web site)

Connect for Kids: www.connectforkids.org

Raising a Daughter: Parents and the Awakening of a Healthy Woman by Jeanne Elium and Don Elium. Ten Speed Press, 2003.

Meeting at the Crossroads by Lyn Mikel Brown and Carol Gilligan. Random House, 1993.

Care About Girls free list serv: join by e-mailing subscribe-careaboutgirls@yahoogroups.com

Things Will Be Different for My Daughter: A Practical Guide to Building Her Self-Esteem and Self-Reliance by Mindy Bingham, and Susan Stryker. Penguin, 1995.

Reviving Ophelia: Saving the Selves of Adolescent Girls by Mary Pipher. Ballantine Books, 1994.

Girls Will Be Girls by Joanne Deak. Hyperion, 2003.

100 Books for Girls to Grow On by Shireen Dodson. HarperPerennial, 1998.

Especially for dads and stepdads:

Dads and Daughters: Inspiring and Supporting Your Daughter As She's Growing Up So Fast by Joe Kelly. Broadway Books, 2002.

Fatherneed: Why Father Care Is As Essential As Mother Care for Your Child by Kyle D. Pruett, MD. Broadway Books, 2001.

The Collected Wisdom of Fathers by Will Glennon. Conari Press, 2003.

Faith of Our Fathers: African-American Men Reflect on Fatherhood by Andre C. Willis. Plume, 1997.

Dads and Daughters: www.dadsanddaughters.org: DadTalk free list serv: Join by e-mailing subscribe-dadtalk@yahoogroups.com

Especially for moms and stepmoms

Between Mother and Daughter by Amanda and Judy Ford. Conari Press, 1999.

Girl in the Mirror: Mothers and Daughters in the Years of Adolescence by Nancy L. Snyderman and Peg Streep. Hyperion, 2003.

Mother Daughter Revolution by Elizabeth Debold, Idelisse Malave, and Marie Wilson. Bantam Doubleday Dell, 1994.

Keep Talking: A Mother-Daughter Guide to the Pre-Teen Years by Lynda Madison. Andrews McMeel, 1997.

Ophelia's Mom: Loving and Letting Go of Adolescent Daughters by Nina Shandler. Crown Publishing, 2001.

Especially for girls

New Moon: www.newmoon.org

www.forgirlsandtheirdreams.org

New Moon books on various topics

American Girl Library Series: nonfiction books on various topics, Pleasant Company Publications.

The Girls' Book of book series by Catherine Dee, Little Brown Children's Books.

The Girls' Guide to Life by Catherine Dee, Little Brown Children's Books, 1997.

INDEX

ABOUT THE AUTHOR

Nancy Gruver is founder and publisher of the groundbreaking international publication, *New Moon®: The Magazine for Girls and Their Dreams.* Gruver is a national leader in the movement to empower girls and foster their creativity and self-confidence. Nancy and *New Moon®* have received many awards: AAUW's Eleanor Roosevelt Award, one of twenty-five Moms We Love by *Working Mother* magazine, the YWCA-USA's Woman Entrepreneur award, the Women of Distinction award from the National Association for Women in Education, and *Parenting* magazine's Parenting Achievement Award. *New Moon®* has garnered seven Parent's Choice Foundation Awards (including Best Children's Magazine, 1995, 1997, 1999, 2000, 2001, and 2003, five Educational Press Association of America Design and Editorial Awards, three MMPA Awards, and the *Utne Reader*'s 1994 Alternative Press Award. She is a frequent speaker and media guest on girls' adolescence and successful strategies for parents and professionals who live and work with girls ages eight and up.